Dr. Gloom's
CRYPT of CURIOSITIES
Take Home Tourist Trap

1st Edition

Edited by
CHRIS & MELISSA LAMARTINA

Written by
CHRIS LAMARTINA, NICK BALDWIN,
RICHARD DONAHUE, MELISSA FOLEY-
KING, TODD GARDNER,
JUSTIN GETKA, DAVE KIEFABER,
ALIX TOBEY SOUTHWICK, MICHAEL
STETTES, PATRICK STORCK, CALVIN VON
CRUSH, & VINCE WILSON

ISBN-13: 978-1984223876

Copyright © 2018 Chris LaMartina
For more information, email: chrislamartina@yahoo.com

or visit Protean Books & Records - 836 Leadenhall St, Baltimore, MD 21230

UNUSUALLY SPECIAL THANKS

This odd little testament to everything strange and bizarre on this earthly plane would not have been possible without the incredible hard work of and unwavering support from the following people:

Matt Benicewicz of Protean Books & Records

The Haunted Cottage

Mark Burchick

Amanda Boutwell

Matthew DeVille

Rick Fisher

Jimmy George

John Higgins

Andrea Kalfas

Matt Lake

Erik Kristopher Myers

Andrew Reamer

Nathan Roberts

Dave Spencer

Katelynn Zimmerman

We could have given you a

TABLE OF CONTENTS

...but where's the fun in that:?

FOREWARD
BY CHRIS LAMARTINA

In October of 2014, my wife Melissa and I were on our honeymoon in New Orleans, Louisiana. During that week in the heartland of voodoo, we took a day trip to the nearby town of Abita Springs—home of the Abita Brewing Company and, more importantly, the Abita Mystery House.

The Abita Mystery House is a strange little tourist trap in the quaint small town where artist/inventor, John Preble had taken a simple old home and turned it into a wild spectacle of outsider art, weird exhibits, and freakish taxidermy.

There was Darryl the Dogagator - Half dog, half alligator!
There was a crashed UFO that destroyed a retro mobile home!
There was a beautiful house of glass shards—perfect for photos!
There was even a miniature jazz funeral, complete with a full band!

It was imaginative and exciting, but more than anything else, it was *inspiring*.

Near the entrance was a plaque that explained how Mr. Preble was moved to create the Mystery House after a trip to a similar tourist trap in New Mexico. Fascinated by that venture, Preble decided he would make his own attraction; over time, the Abita Mystery House was born.

At that moment, I felt a strong kinship to the old guy and a new dream was born for me. I decided then and there that it would be my goal that when I retired. Melissa and I would turn part of our house into an oddities/curiosities museum. Of course, that would be at least forty years from that moment… or so I thought.

Fate has a funny way of completely messing up your plans.

It started with my buddy, Matt Benicewicz. He contacted me after he started renting a huge warehouse in Baltimore's Federal Hill neighborhood to re-open his business, Protean Books & Records.

Matt knew I made monster movies and suggested I shoot a project at the vast location he had just leased. I stewed on it, but I wasn't actively making anything at that moment. Then, the universe gave me a unique gift.

While visiting Melissa's parents in Lewes, Delaware, we passed by a home-made wooden sign that read, "Dr. Gloom's Crypt of Curiosities." Even though it looked like an invitation to murder, I couldn't pass up such a bizarre opportunity, so I steered the car left and introduced myself to one of the most unique personalities I'd ever met.

There was a sign on the garage that told me to knock on the front door. Ms. Bartolli came out. Geena "Mean Geen" Bartolli was a tough, no-nonsense old lady who ran an oddities shop out of her garage. She was as enthusiastic as she was downright insane. We connected immediately.

Clad in army boots and a faded sundress, the fiery old soul with a big white mop top barked at us about the rules of the Crypt.

As we ventured into the musty old shack, I was astounded by the sheer tenacity of Ms. Bartolli and I pressed for more information. She unraveled the full story of how the Crypt came to be and I confided in Ms. Bartolli that one day, we would love to run a similar museum.

We stayed there for hours until the setting sun made our departure imminent, but you see, I never left those exhibits.

Ole Mean Geen put her hand on my shoulder as we departed and explained that we might be the last folks to ever go inside the Crypt. She was fixing to retire and had grown a little too old to keep up with marketing the operation. She had bought the lot of oddities on a whim, and now it didn't seem right for her to run it any longer.

In a moment that I will never forget, she looked me in the eye and asked me what I would do if she gifted me the contents of her garage. I remembered Matt offering his warehouse for a film shoot. I explained the opportunity. We could move the Crypt to the weird city of Baltimore, and creeps from all around would visit the spot when they grew sick of boring tourist schtick like the Inner Harbor.

Mean Geen looked me up and down. She cracked a smirk that revealed half a mouth of gold teeth. She shook my hand and told me to come back the following weekend with a U-Haul truck.

The rest is history.

ABOUT THE CRYPT

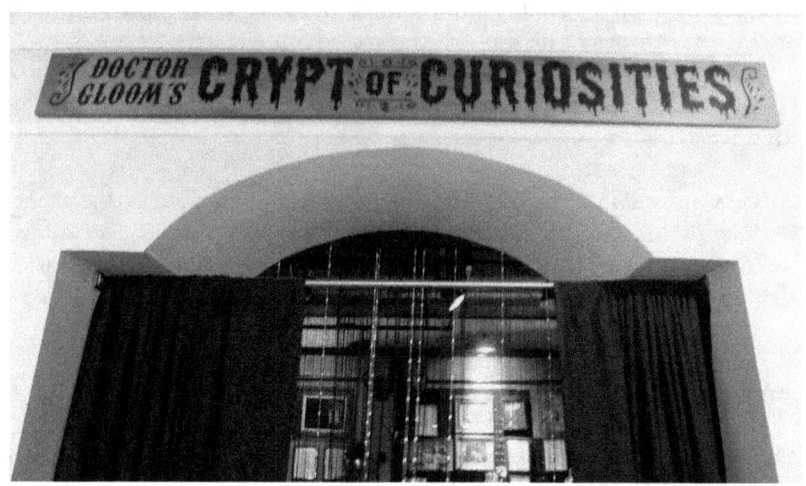

Greetings! Thank you for your interest in the Crypt of Curiosities, the beloved life's work of Dr. Augustus Gloom.

Born in Terre Haute, Indiana in 1917, Gloom was intrigued by the strange and unusual from a very young age. His morbid interest in death customs and bizarre tribal rituals lead his fellow students at Adamson University to refer to him as "Gloomy Gus." With this morose moniker adopted proudly, Gloom doubled down on his peculiar hobbies and began to amass the most incredible collection of outlandish artifacts in the continental United States.

The original Crypt of Curiosities was first opened in 1954 in Greencastle, Indiana. While Dr. Gloom worked toward his PhD in Archeology, his sister Beatrice attended to the daily operations of the museum. It remained in Greencastle until the spring of 1977, when Dr. Gloom was killed in a freak ferris wheel accident while on a sideshow gaffe buying expedition in the town of Sturgis, Michigan.

Beatrice Gloom sold the entire collection to the public library of Elm Buff, Alabama. The collection stayed in storage for a decade when it was purchased by notable cryptozoology enthusiast, Geena "Mean Geen"

Bartolli. Independently wealthy Delaware native Bartolli converted her garage into what would become the modern Crypt of Curiosities. For decades, she gave small-group tours to eager tourists from around the world.

In the winter of 2015, Bartolli met the current curator, horror filmmaker Chris LaMartina. Impressed by his motion picture, *Call Girl of Cthulhu* and his clearly Sicilian surname, she asked LaMartina if he would be interested in maintaining the museum upon her retirement. LaMartina agreed on the condition that he could relocate the museum to his hometown of Baltimore, MD. When a space became available in the backroom of Protean Books & Records, LaMartina made the necessary arrangements to open the fourth incarnation of the beloved Crypt of Curiosities.

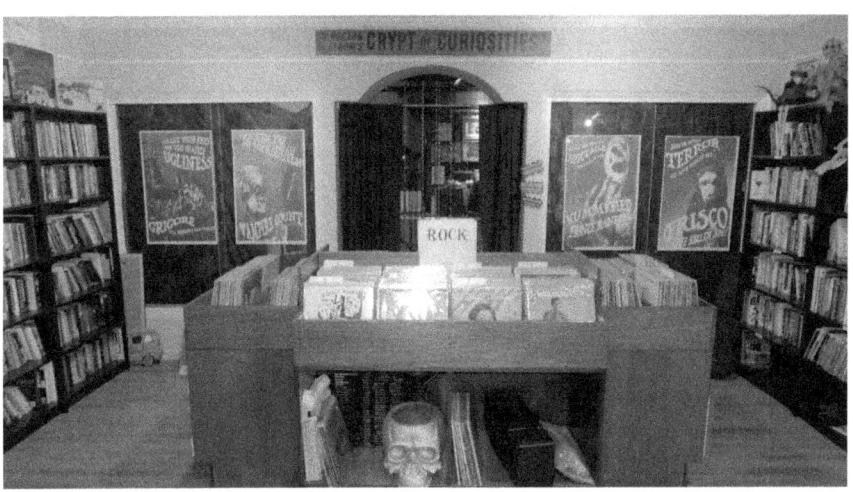

THE MUMMIFIED
PRINCE RANEFER

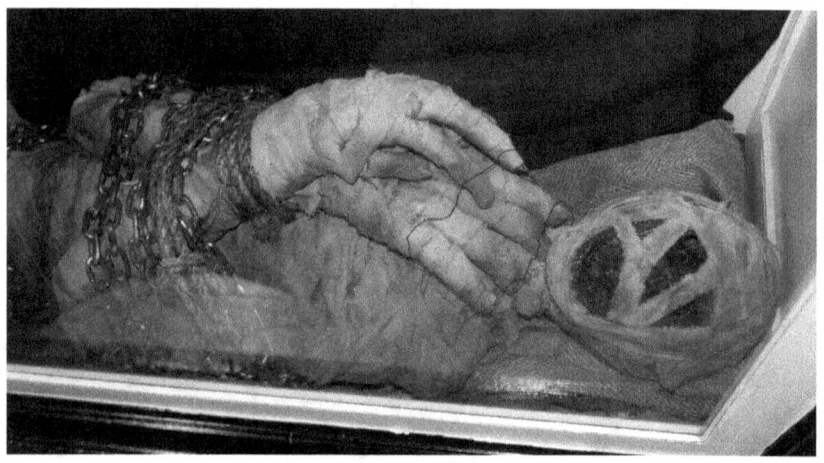

Ranefer, son of Pharaoh Sneferu (aka Soris) of the Fourth Dynasty of the Old Kingdom of Egypt, served as his father's "Overseer," advising on such subjects as finances, crops, and divination, since all were considered intertwined.

From early childhood, his elongated features were thought to represent an influential pull from both the heavens (overseen by the sun god Ra) and the underworld Duat (held by the god Osiris).

His extended fingers were seen as divining rods of prognostication. Due to the deformity his writings were sparse and hard-created, but they were typically written with much consideration, helping further his image and station.

These remains are considered the best preserved example of O.K.— 4th K mummification techniques.

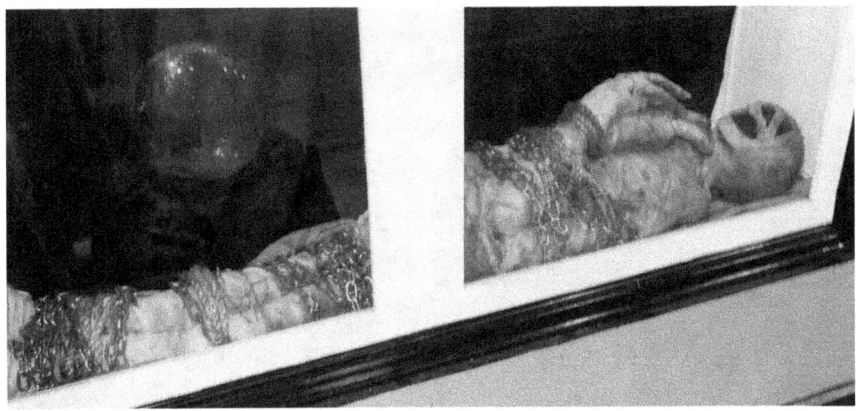

It is unclear how this mummy came into Dr. Gloom's possession. It was reported stolen from at the Ewing Scientific Museum of Scotland in 1927, but since then, that institution had closed and the family of Mr. Ewing (a well-known philanthropist) would not accept its gracious return from Dr. Gloom. Instead, Ewing decided its "natural" home would be in the Crypt.

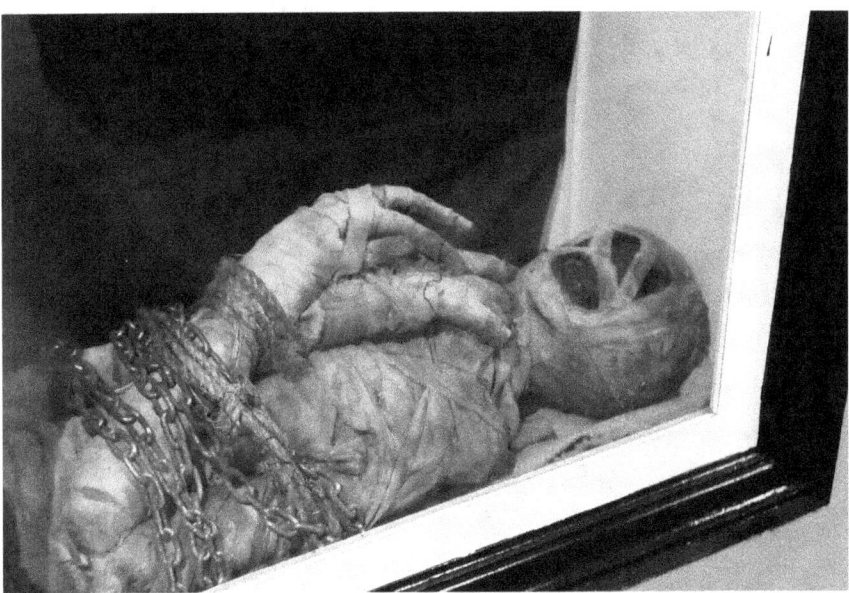

HARBOR WITCH

The Harbor of Baltimore, founded in that most prosperous year of our Lord 1632, was stricken with haunt. The sinister phantasm known as the "Harbor Witch" stalked these local waters.

The Witch was the wife of a successful merchant who came to Baltimore shortly after its founding.

She was a troublesome woman, able to calculate numbers without pen and paper. She flaunted this ability among men, demonstrating it without the proper shame and humility befitting a servant of God. When her talents caused trouble for the annual census, a public hearing was called, in which she alleged that her count was more accurate than that of the official census-taker.

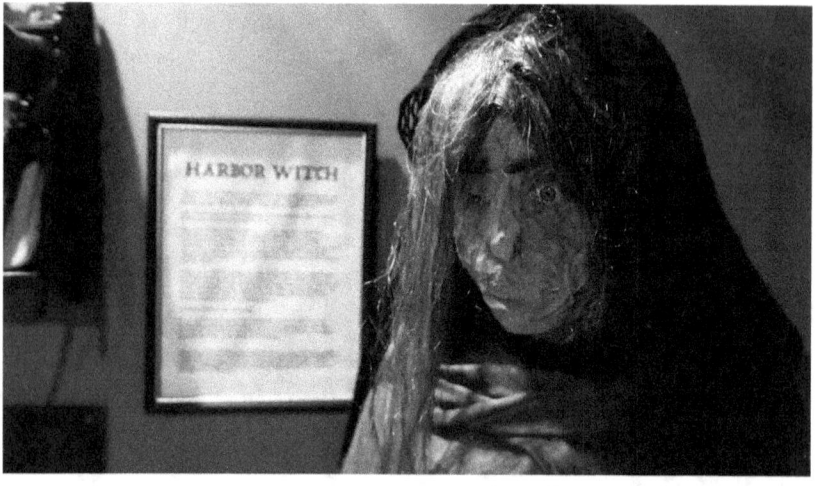

When proof of this allegation was demanded of her, she began reciting clots of raw numbers that, to the ears of all who bore witness, took the form of Satan's hideous dark speech, bereft of truth and sealed at the edges with lies. She was found guilty of heresy and cast into the Harbor as the first official act of the newly-established Port of Baltimore.

In those waters, she drowned.

It is said that her spirit still treads the waters of the Harbor, endlessly pointing and counting in a foul attempt to take the census. If you see her, and she points at you without a number passing her lips, your death is imminent.

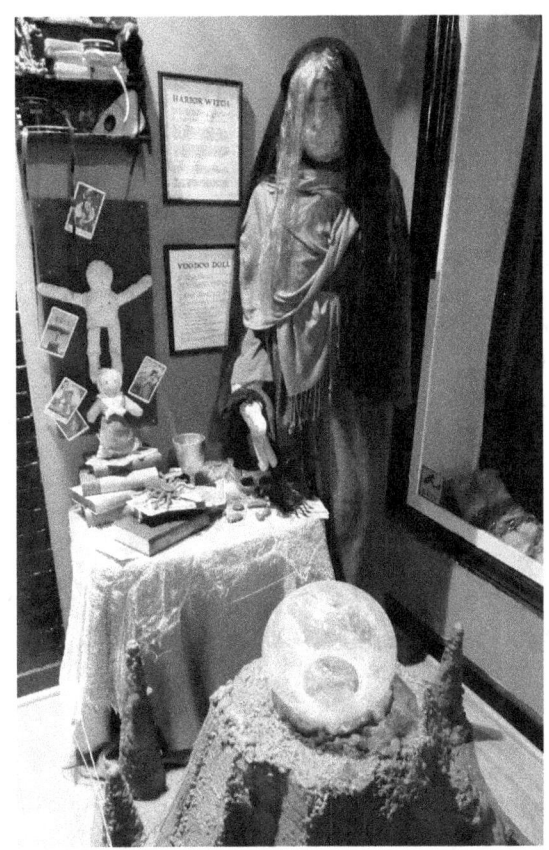

The Crypt of Curiosities understands this woman was not a witch—rather, she was an intelligent woman murdered for her intellect in a time that punished empowered females. We also acknowledge that our portrayal in wax is not historically accurate in regard to her lifestyle or likeness.

This figure was sculpted by a local artisan who blatantly ignored a reference painting graciously included in the folklore tome, Roughneck Rogues from Baltimore's Past. first published in 1817.

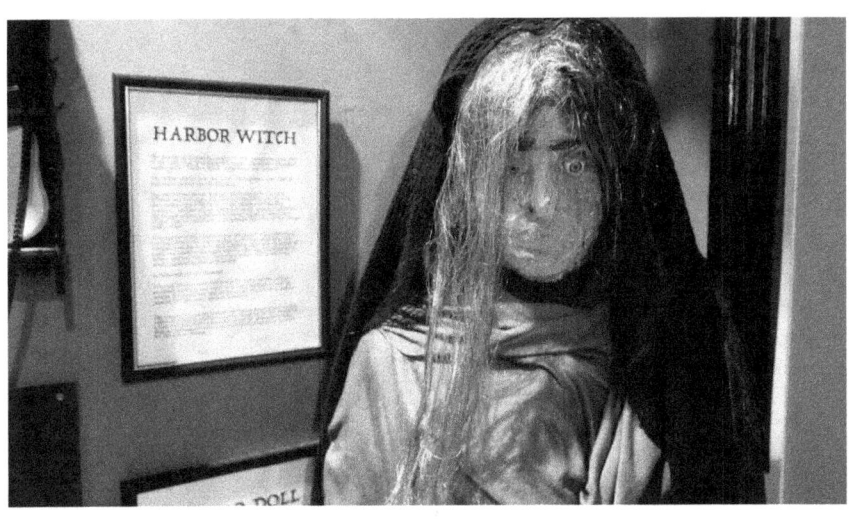

VOODOO DOLL

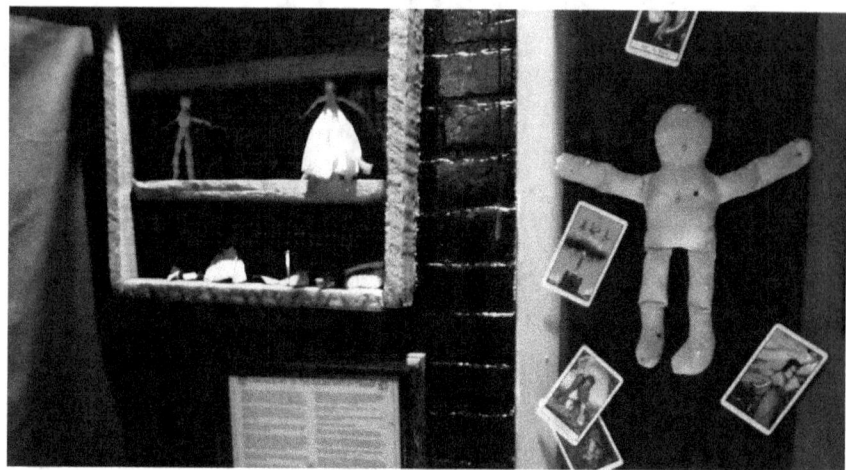

The Voodoo doll is a form of gris-gris, a ritualized form of invoking the spirits to act in a defined way toward a targeted person.

Voodoo means "spirit of God." Believers in voodoo hold true to one distant yet ever-present God, yet they speak with the spirits, called the Loa. The Loa are our dead ancestors and the messengers of the Creator.

The doll can be used for love, for power and domination, for luck, for uncrossing and, though most practitioners caution against it, for harm.

The color of the doll has very strong inclinations for its intended purpose:

- **White** – positive, purification, or healing
- **Red** – love, attraction, or power
- **Green** – growth, wealth, money, and fertility
- **Yellow** – success and confidence
- **Purple** – spirit realm, wisdom, or psychic exploration
- **Blue** – love and peace
- **Black** – to dispel negative energy or to summon it

These seven colors are also found on pins and needles. They are stuck into the doll to emphasize the intention.

DEVIL HAWK OF AMCHITKA ISLAND

On May 2, 1974, Cpt. Tim Calverton and his crew were fishing off the coast of Amchitka Island, AL, when they received a distress call from another fishing vessel, the Trenchant, claiming to be under attack by a "black sky of demon birds."

Upon boarding the Trenchant, Calverton's crew found no survivors and no sign of the birds in question, save for one—this specimen—which had become ensnared in the ship's rigging.

Calverton suffered the loss of his left eye and right hand in retrieving the bird; nevertheless, he named it "Ernie" and kept it as a pet.

Both Calverton and Ernie died of natural causes in 1981. Ernie was donated to the Crypt by Susan Calverton.

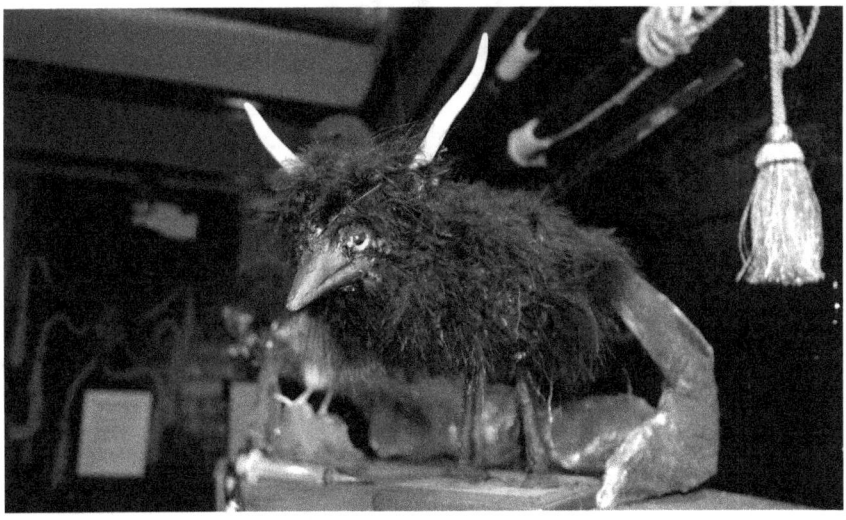

Biologists speculate that Ernie's distinct mutation may have been influenced by nuclear tests that took place on Amchitka throughout the 60s and early 70s. They have been unable to verify this claim as the U.S. Department of Defense has banned all travel to the island.

FIJI MERMAIDS

The Fiji Mermaids below are from two very unique sources.

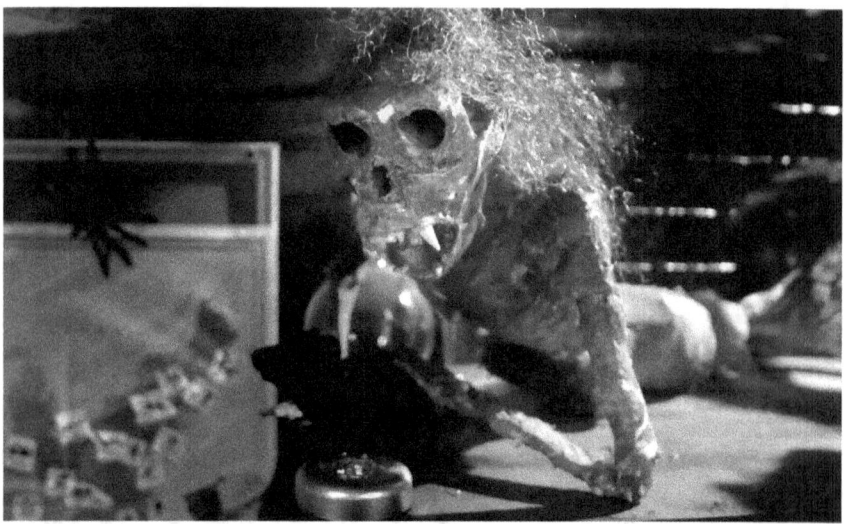

Exhibit A was originally acquired in 1826 by American sea captain Rutherford Penniferd. While cruising along the Japanese coast, Captain Penniferd docked his ship at a small fishing village. Upon reaching land, Penniferd explored the small town and came across a dreary street corner where some Japanese sailors were laughing around a bizarre discovery.

The sailors claimed the dead sea creature was incredibly rare... a mermaid of some sort. Captain Penniferd demanded they sell the uncanny beast. After much negotiating, the deal was settled for three barrels of whiskey, four feathered hats, and a jar of buttons.

Upon return to the States, Captain Penniferd had the animal stuffed and displayed in his church's basement. He charged a five cent admission to any doubtful parishioners who dared to go face-to-face with the "Devil." It remained in that collection until 1998, when the Crypt purchased it at the congregation's rummage sale.

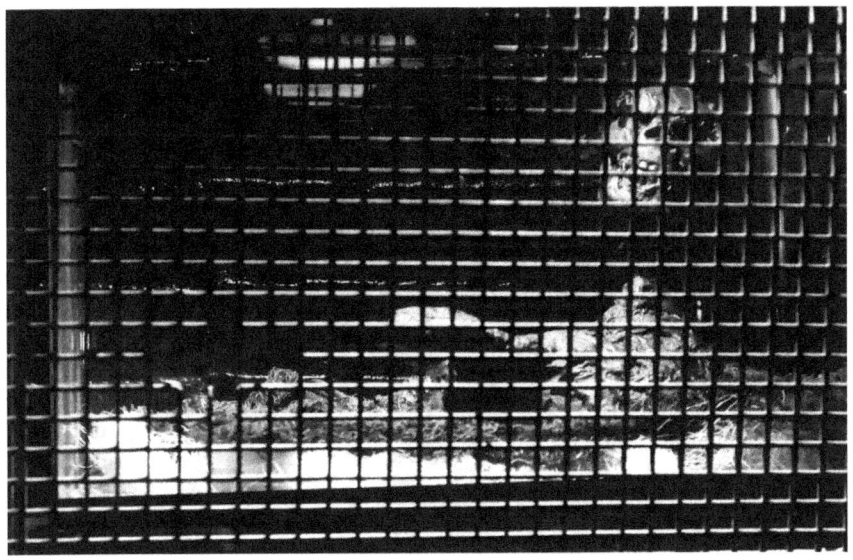

Exhibit B was donated to us under truly unusual circumstances.

One rainy Sunday morning in 2014, a weather-worn crate was delivered to the front steps of the Crypt. There was no name and no return address. When the box was opened, the only contents were this skeletal Fiji Mermaid, a half eaten container of fish food, and a tattered hand-written note asking for compassion and guidance in the upbringing of their scaly offspring. However, it was too late to be saved. The unfortunate creature was named Phineas.

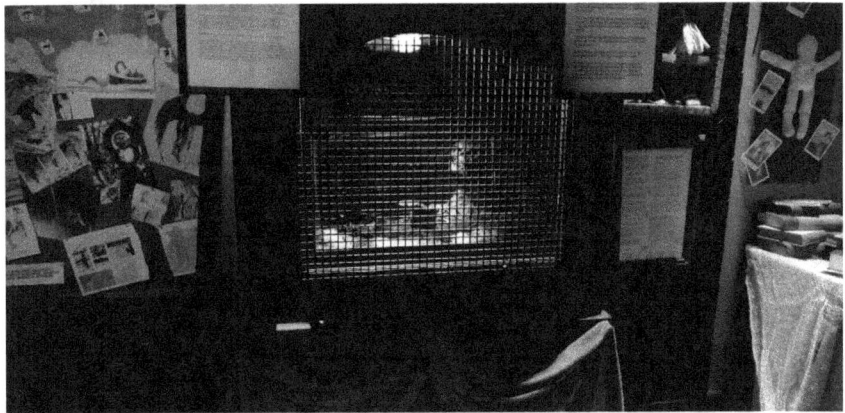

BRUNO
THE HEADLESS DUCK

On September 10, 1945, farmer Lloyd Olsen of Fruita, Colorado was planning to eat supper with his mother-in-law and was sent out to the yard by his wife to bring back a chicken. Olsen chose a five-and-a-half-month-old Wyandotte chicken named Mike. The axe removed the bulk of the head but missed the jugular vein, leaving one ear and most of the brain stem intact.

Due to Olsen's failed attempt to behead Mike, the chicken was still able to balance on a perch and walk clumsily. He attempted to preen, peck for food, and crow, though with limited success; his "clucking" consisted of a gurgling sound made in his throat.

When Mike did not die, Olsen instead decided to care for the bird. He fed it a mixture of milk and water via an eyedropper, and gave it small grains of corn. The chicken lived for 17 more months until a corn kernel got lodged in his throat and he choked to death.

Bruno, the headless duck before you, was not as lucky.

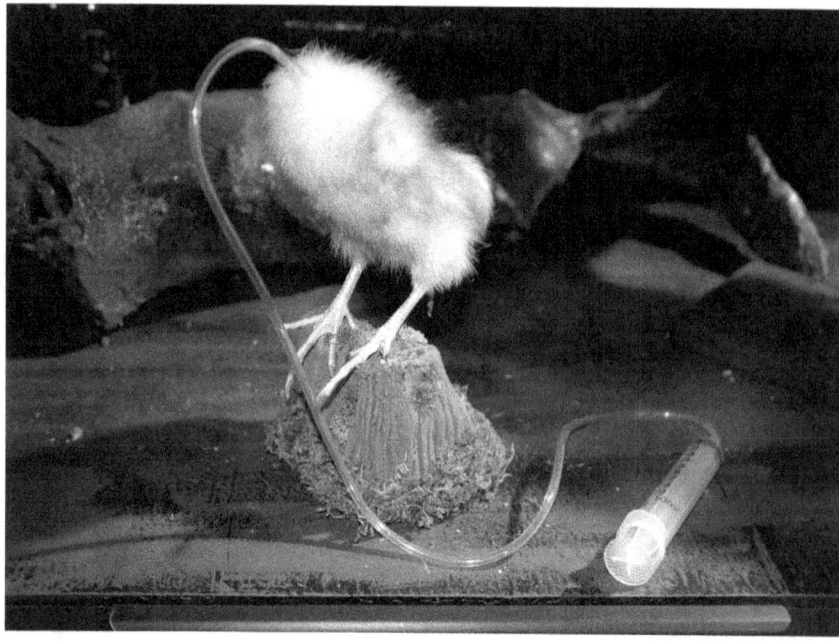

In 1946, Italian Lucio Passeri, had recently immigrated to the United States in hope of raising ducks. When Passeri heard of Olsen's remarkable, carnival-traveling headless chicken, he decided he could follow Olsen's lead. Passeri began experimenting on his animals by practicing sustainable living techniques after their decapitation.

After dozens of failed "experiments," Passeri perfected his operation with Bruno here. The syringe below was used to feed the critter after oral delivery was no longer possible.

Sadly, Bruno only lived a very short time after having his head severed—just long enough for a summer engagement at a Coney Island sideshow.

The Crypt was gifted this piece by dear friend and brother in weirdness, Calvin Von Crush during the spring of 2017.

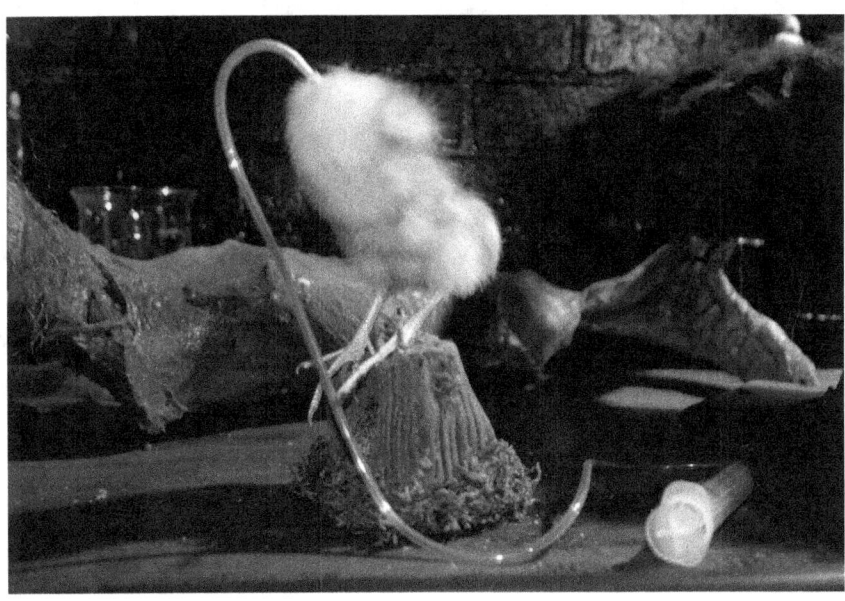

SHIPWRECK REMNANTS

BROKEN OAR

This splintered oar was found washed up on the rocks near George's Island in Nova Scotia, Canada. It belonged to the S.S. Haig, a privately-owned noncommercial fishing vessel owned by Mr. Lawrence Q. Bradley. Bradley had been hired by amateur cryptozoologist Brenda Hoffsetter, who wanted to explore the region for evidence of the storied sea beast: the Bannen Water Banshee. In old pirate lore, it was a siren-like serpent rumored to swim along the dark waters.

The recovered ship's log provided little information, except that Hoffsetter believed some type of large sea creature was, in fact, tracking along with the ship. No living passengers were discovered when authorities located the boat.

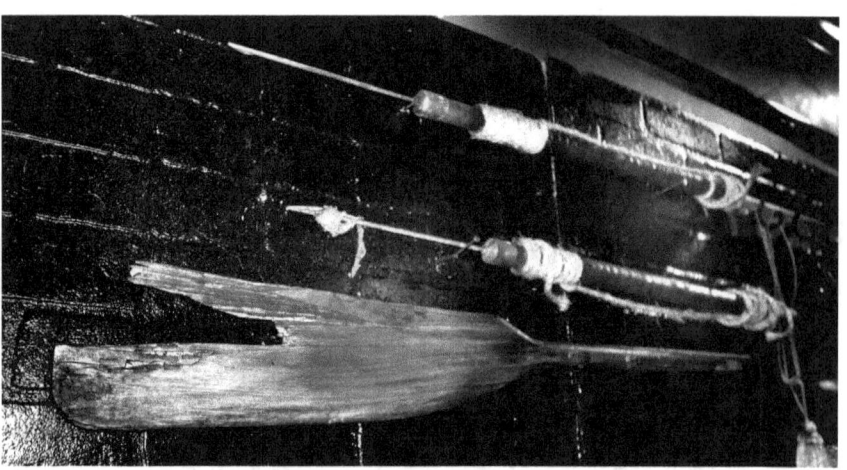

HARPOONS

These rusty harpoons were originally used on the Victrosa whaling ship during a trip through the Bering Strait in 1894. They were used as evidence in the mass murder trial of Russian Captain Anar Vagus, who went crazy during the voyage. Vargas claimed that the murderous voices of shipwrecked souls demanded he and his entire crew join their army in the netherworld. When the ship arrived back on shore, authorities arrested Vargas for having dismembered his entire crew.

THE GRISLY REMAINS OF BARON RADU
(the Eschede Vampire)

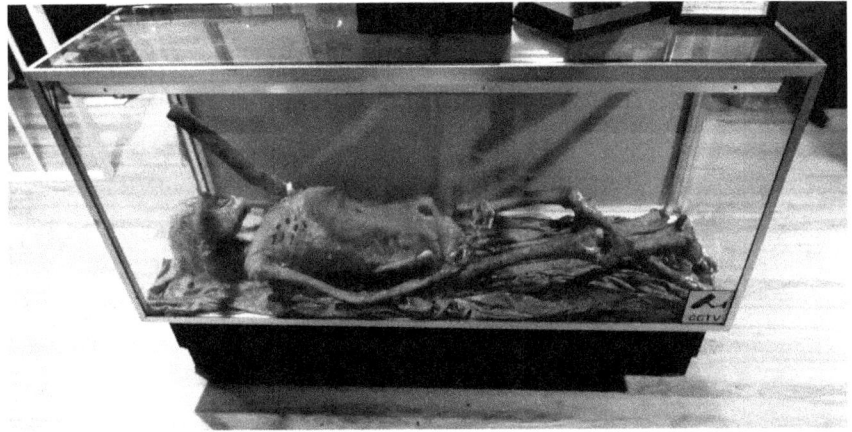

Peer into this glass case and feast your eyes on Baron Radu Von Blutsauger (1742–1807). Blutsauger was a German nobleman who lived near the village of Eschede in the Celle district of Lower Saxony.

As the legend goes, the Baron's dark descent into the world of vampirism began on a cold fall evening in 1807. While hunting for wild game, Radu came upon a cluster of ancient ruins… a desolate location where witches reportedly communed with Satan himself. The other nobility with the Baron knew the circle was used for the "Black Mass" and refused to hunt there. Radu laughed off their superstitions and continued to hunt when they parted ways.

Days later, Radu was found dead near the edge of the forest—his entire body drained of blood. Shortly after, he was given a lavish funeral, a spectacular event fitting a nobleman of his stature.

Servants at Castle Blutsauger expressed concern that someone resembling the Baron was seen in the courtyard in the weeks after the funeral, and it was not long after these sightings that the Baron's wife and his four children fell ill, succumbing weeks later to a rare blood disease.

After the family was buried, the peasants of Eschede were convinced their superstitions were correct. They stormed the Blutsauger family crypt and opened the vault to find the bodies perfectly preserved— except for Baron Radu's.

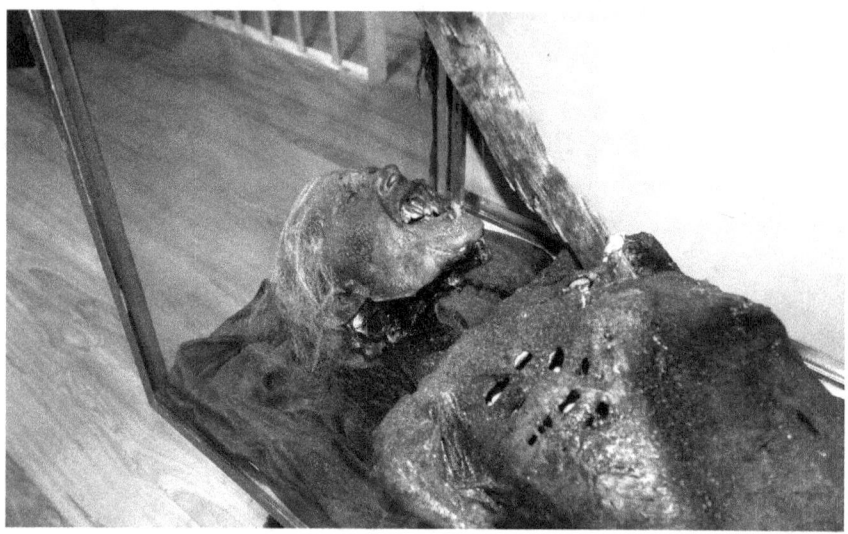

Radu's body was bloated, as if he had gorged upon food. His hair and fingernails had grown as well, and crimson blood trickled from his lips. The peasants believed the Baron had become a vampire, and they had no other

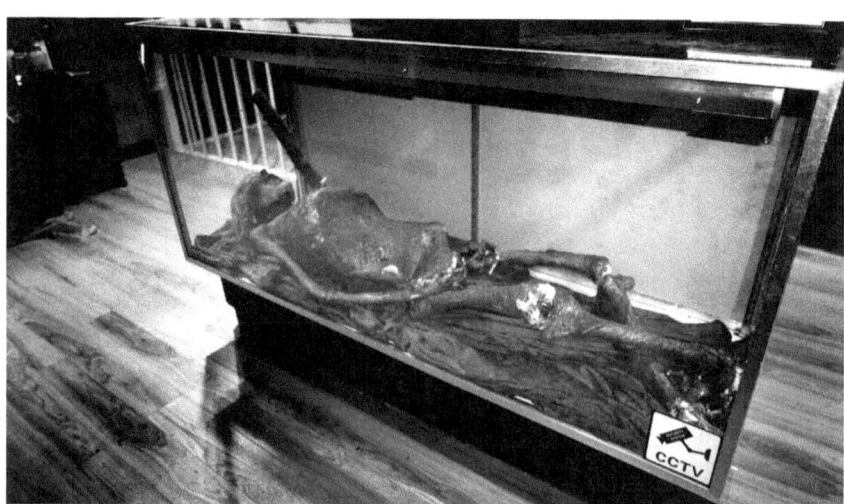

choice but to put a stake through the heart of each family member in the vault.

It was said that when the stake went through the Baron's heart, he let out a blood curdling scream.

Radu's grisly remains were long believed to be destroyed, until 1952, when a crate adorned with Blutsauger family crest showed up at an Argentinian estate sale. It moved around among private collectors until we were gifted it in 2015 by Vince Wilson, formerly of the Haunted Cottage in Harper's Ferry, WV.

The only condition of the donation was that we keep the wooden stake buried in the Baron's chest as long as he was in our possession.

We agreed.

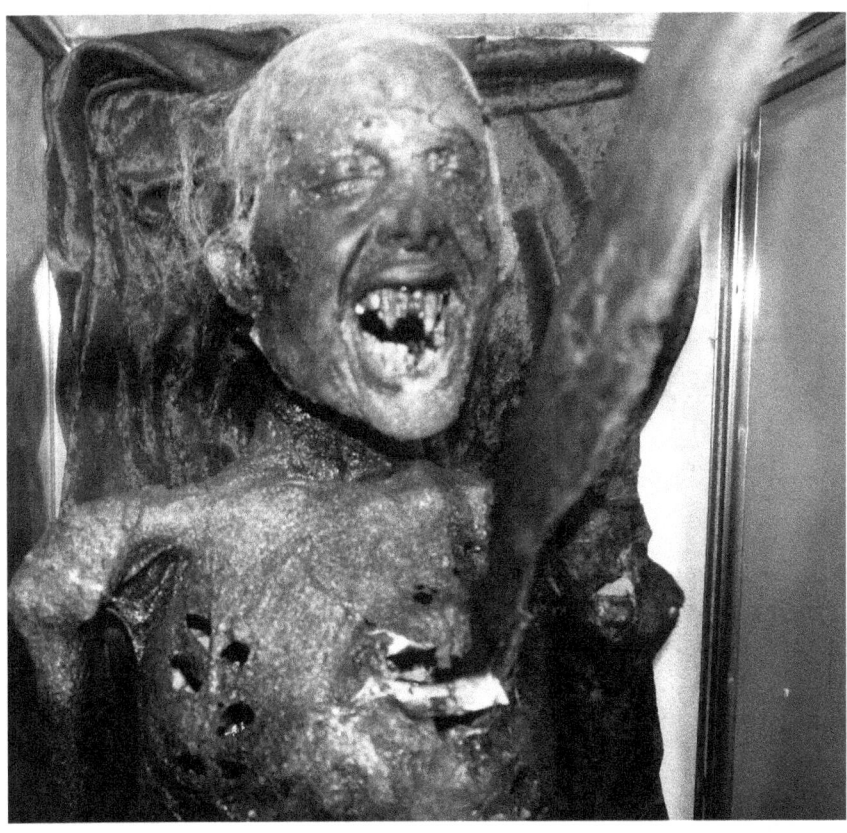

LAVERNE LAKE MONSTER

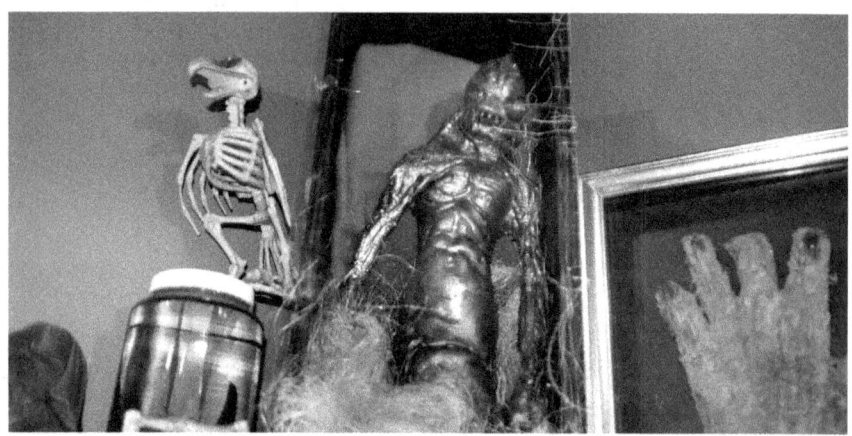

Discovered in 1962 by a corn farmer in Hay Springs, Nebraska, the Laverne Lake Monster was believed to be a direct result of pesticide run off, which coincidentally contributed to its preservation.

The green glow of the creature's scales was studied by members of the biology department at Sheridan Valley Community College. The physical handling of the animal lead to some peculiar circumstances that were never fully realized, even fifty years after the strange happenings.

Handlers of the fish-like creature grew bizarre skin lesions that resembled sparkling scales. After a few days of increased irritation, the infected students and faculty developed an intense thirst for salt water.

One of the patients, freshman Sarah Espinosa, died from the painful bacteria only weeks after contracting the disease. The other three parties eventually recovered in the ensuing months and showed no further warning signs of the disease.

In fact, one of the patients, sophomore Buddy Eisner, went on to win a bronze medal for swimming during the 1968 Olympics in Mexico City Mexico.

HAND *of* GLORY

The Hand of Glory is the dried and pickled hand of a man who has been hanged, often specified as being the left (Latin: *sinister*) hand or, if the man were hanged for murder, the hand that "did the deed."

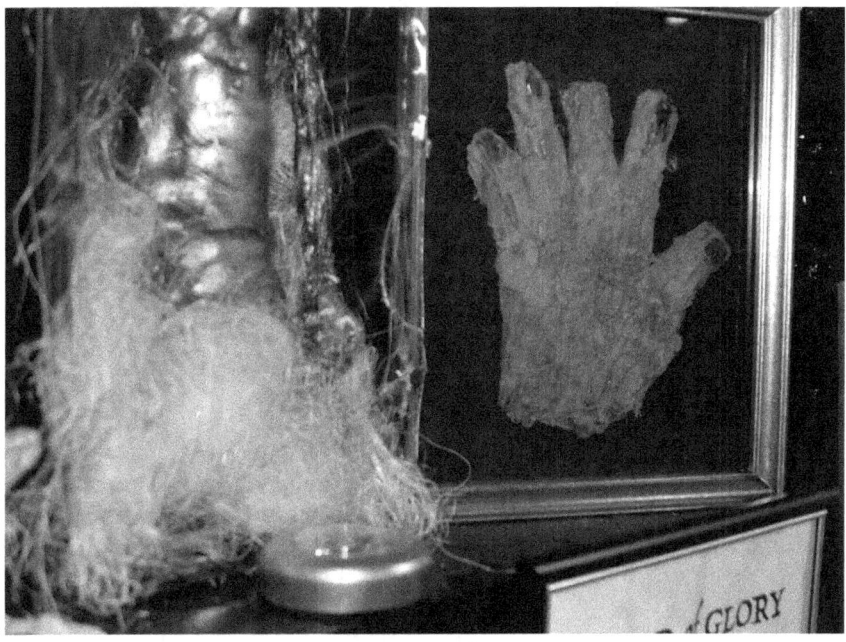

Old European beliefs attribute great powers to a Hand of Glory combined with a candle made from fat from the corpse of the same malefactor who died on the gallows. The candle so made, lighted, and placed in the Hand of Glory, is said to render motionless all persons to whom it is presented.

According to legend, the candle can be put out only with milk and only gives light to the holder. The Hand of Glory also purportedly has the power to unlock any door the bearer encounters.

THE BALTIMORE GYPSY MURDER

On November 16, 1994, Douglas Thomas Clark brutally murdered and then decapitated a 62-year-old palm reader and fortune teller, Sister Myra, in her storefront home located at 4006 Pulaski Highway.

Myra, born Deborah Stevens, was the daughter of King Dick Stevens, the last of the great Gypsy kings. The Stevens clan was a powerful family in America as far back as the 1920s.

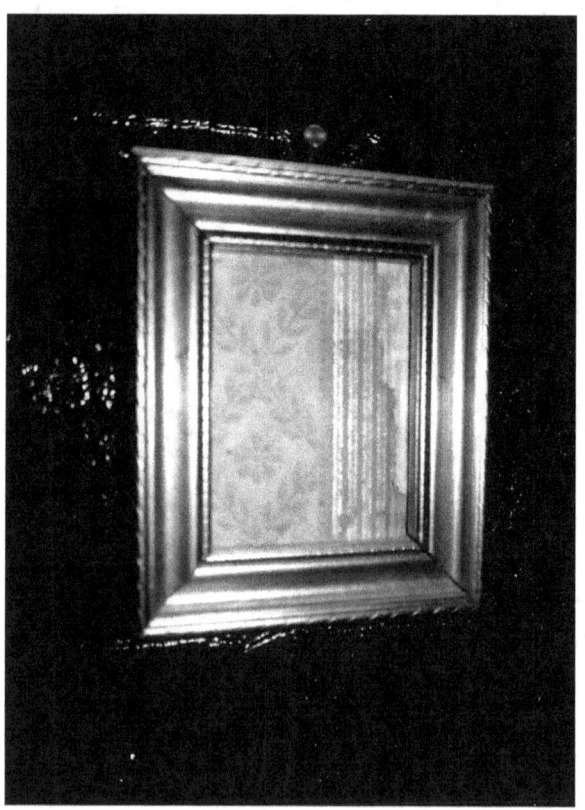

The convicted murderer, Clark, believed that Sister Myra had placed a hex upon him, and he hoped that killing her would undo any type of curse.

After committing the crime, Clark attempted suicide numerous times and was eventually placed in a mental health facility until 2003, when he was released to his mother's care.

This piece of wallpaper was removed on September 12, 2016 from the hallway in which the headless corpse was found.

MR. WESLEY'S ASSISTANT

For years, the middle schoolers at Springer Prep School in Dayton, Ohio, thought math teacher Ronald Wesley was a psychic of sorts. He always knew exactly when one of the students was misbehaving, whether they were cheating on a test or about to fire a snot-laced spit ball.

It was almost as if he had eyes in the back of his head, *and that wasn't too far from the truth…*

The outward appearance of Ronald Wesley shows nothing "freakish." In fact, the common observer would have no idea that Ronald Wesley was actually one of a pair of Siamese twins.

Ronald and Donald Wesley were born February 2, 1922, and doctors were worried that separating the brothers would lead to Donald's demise.

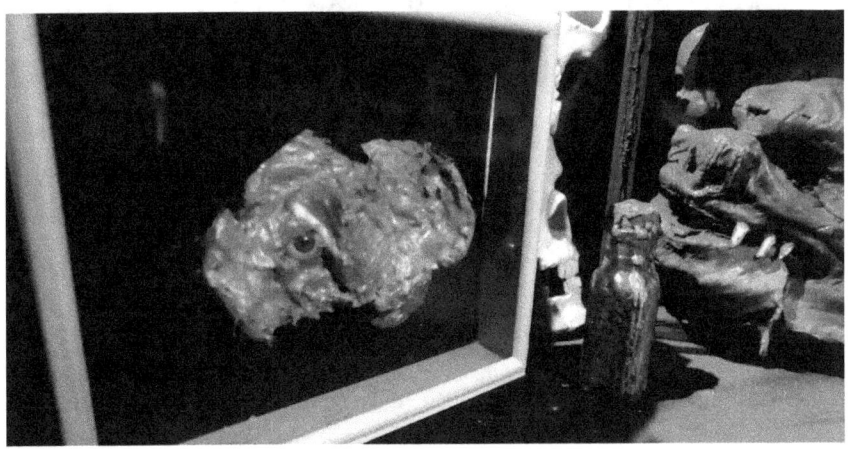

Ronald's conjoined twin, Donald, was simply a grotesque face that grew from the back of his right shoulder. Donald had eyes, ears, and a nose. His mouth was ill-formed and he shared a stomach (and also a brain) with his twin brother. Unwilling to exploit his poor misfortune, Ronald rarely spoke about his brother for financial gain, but they did often have fun at the expense of friends, most notably with magic tricks.

Sadly, in 1958, Ronald suffered a fatal sinus infection that eventually lead to the death of both twins. Knowing that a meager teacher's salary could not take care of funeral expenses, Ronald preemptively sold his brother's face to be preserved through taxidermy for "scientific benefit."

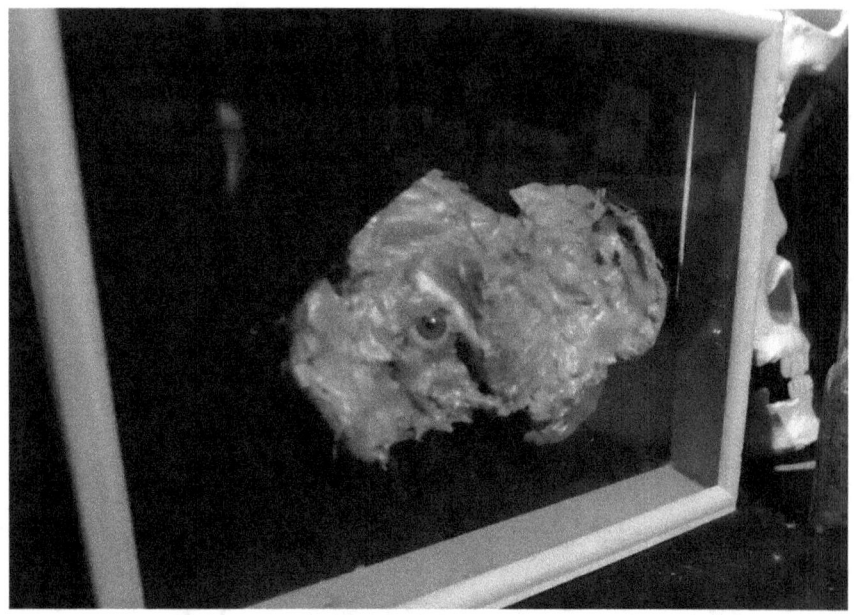

Donald's face was donated to the Crypt in 2016, upon the retirement of Morgantown huckster, Colonel Zane Channell, who previously ran the West Virginia fun house, the Colonel's Mad House of Lively Amusements.

CLAIRVOYANT'S BRAIN

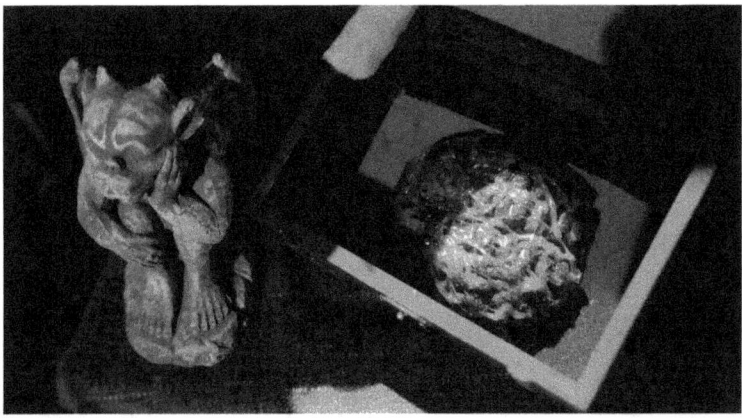

Enclosed are the partial cerebral remains of Jeron Woodworth, a London-born clairvoyant who was briefly employed by the government of Myanmar, where he served as an adviser to Than Shwe.

Claiming to see into the future, Woodworth made a name for himself as a television personality and provided spiritual and strategic counsel to Shwe, whose military junta had seized control of Myanmar.

That job, and his life, ended in 2008 when the psychic predicted that Cyclone Nargis would bypass the country entirely, communicating Shwe's benevolent leadership in so doing.

Contrary to Woodworth's prediction, the storm made landfall in Myanmar in May 2008, killing 140,000 people and displacing as many as 2 million. Worse, the storm came just as Shwe was rigging an election to approve a new constitution, and Shwe's government was exposed as a human rights crisis on the global stage.

Woodworth was promptly arrested, imprisoned in a brutal jungle gulag, and executed.

The reason behind extracting Woodworth's brain is unclear, as is the precise method of extraction, but rumors suggest that Shwe intended to display it as a warning for the other members of his cabinet. These remains were kept by a prison guard and eventually sold to an American collector, who bequeathed them to the Crypt upon his death.

SINISTER SPALA SNAKE
SHED SKIN & TRIBAL ART

Below, you will see the only skin ever found of the elusive sinister Spala Snake, named for both its vengeful tendencies and also the Polish town from which its discoverer (and first documented victim), Jaropelk Horodecki, hailed.

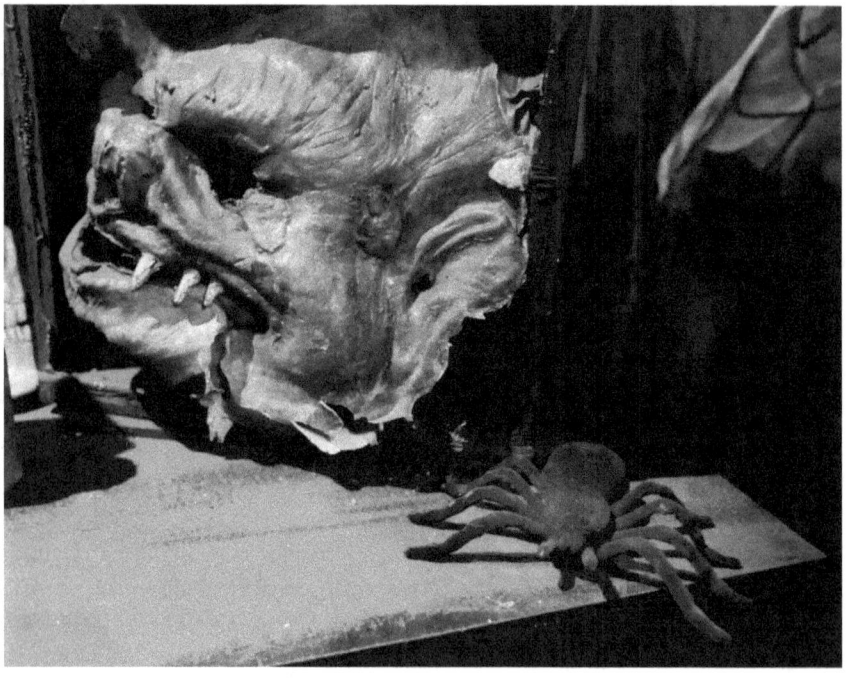

While Spala make their home in the remote recesses of the Amazon jungle, recent human autopsy reports from the Falkland islands bearing descriptions of the Spala's signature bite indicate the presence of the snakes, likely brought there as stowaways transported by shipping vessels.

Underneath this passage, you will see a unique Amazonian tribal artifact. This craftsman's carving, produced sometime in the early 19th century, depicts the fierce head and multiple rope-like tails of the Spala.

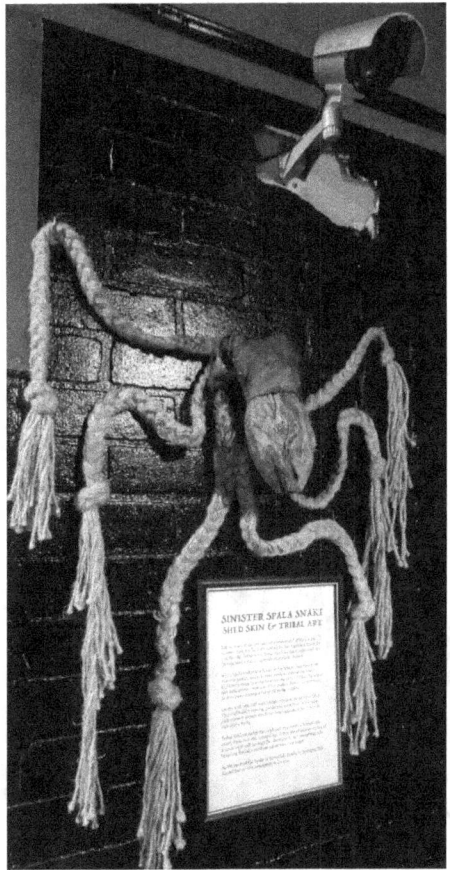

Tribal folklore states that each tail represents a human vice: greed, hate, lust, etc. Legend has it that the ritualistic eating of a Spala's tail will prevent the devourer from committing acts based on the tail's corresponding vice ever again.

As the meat of the Spala is incredibly deadly to humans, this legend has proven repeatedly to be true.

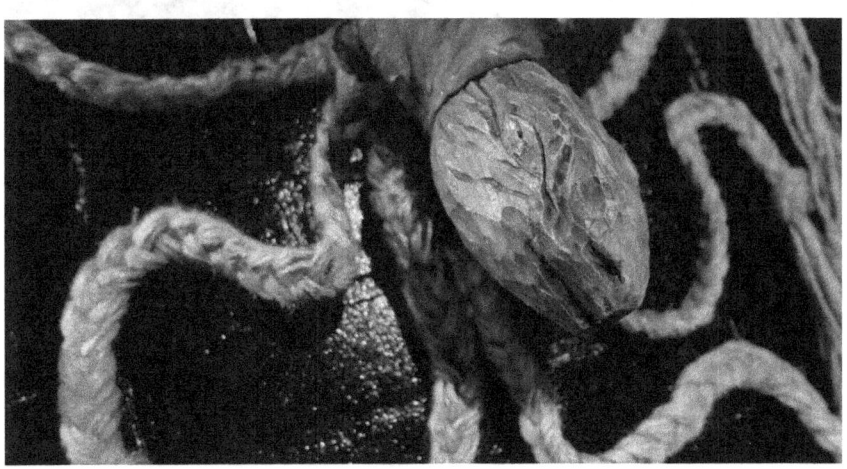

OLD SCRATCH
the Ventriloquist's Dummy

Perhaps you've never heard of Thomas Walker, the Fundamentalist Ventriloquist who travelled the Bible Belt circuit in the 1930s, touting a vaudeville act filled with homespun humor and quaint moral lessons, but you surely heard of his partner... who's known by many names.

Walker and his religious routine quietly traversed the South and Midwest unnoticed until one night in Hazlehurst, Mississippi, when a freak thunderstorm changed everything.

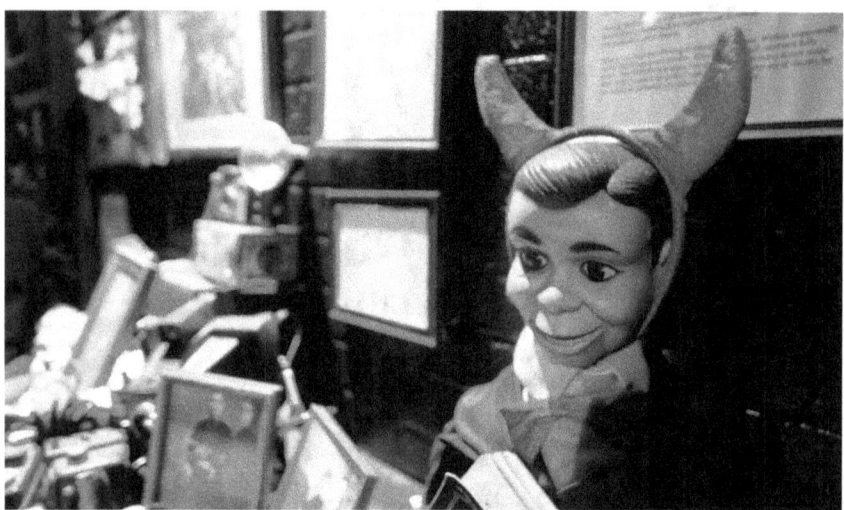

In later testimonies, Walker claimed that his dummy, Nicky, began to speak to him behind closed doors and demanded he therefore be referred to as "Old Scratch." Knowing that the new moniker was the name for the Devil himself, Thomas Walker refused. The dummy was not satisfied, and that's when things went downhill fast.

When left alone, Walker claimed that Old Scratch would rip pages from his Bible, turn crosses upside down, and scribble Satanic symbols on the walls.

During their routine, Old Scratch would throw his voice at someone in the audience, making poor saps scream in strange tongues then fall to the ground in convulsions.

After a few months of trying to salvage his career, Walker supposedly threw Old Scratch in a bonfire. Somehow, the doll returned fully intact. The diabolical dummy changed hands many times until it ended up at the Crypt through a tender act of charity by the estate of eccentric toy collector, Charles Goyer.

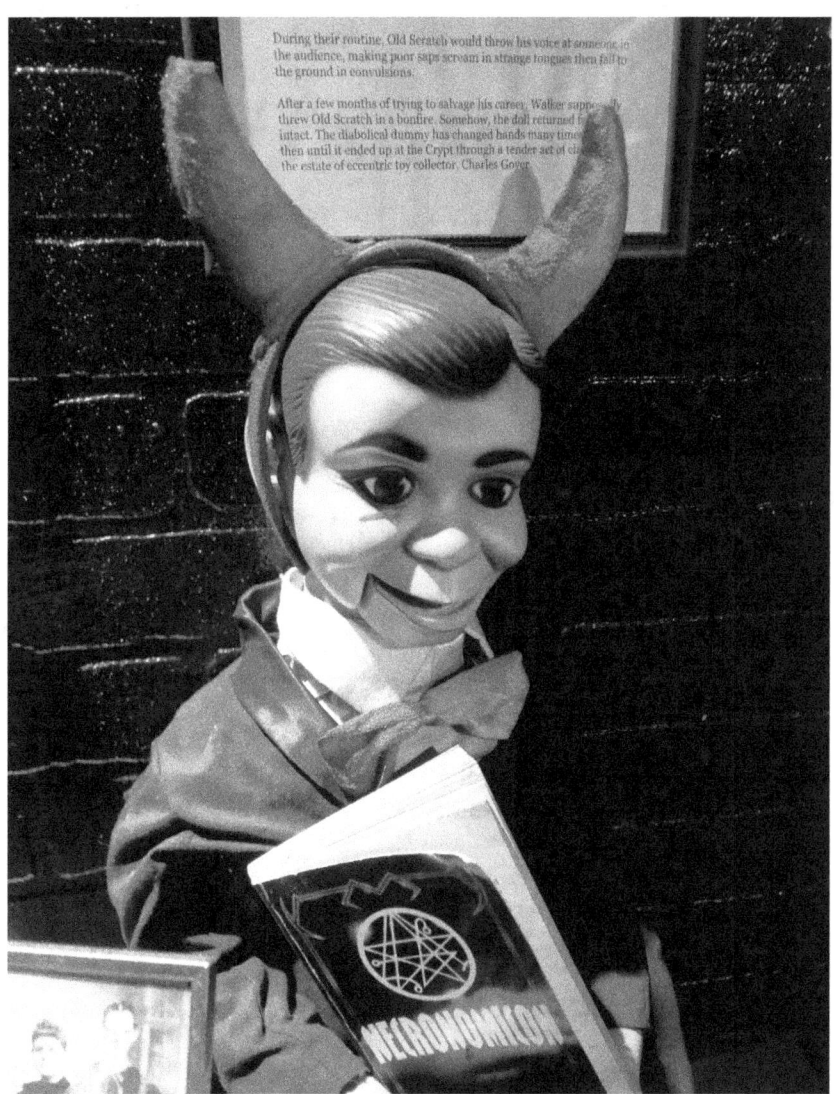

SPIRIT PHOTOGRAPHY

They say a picture's worth a thousand words, but these are worth a thousand screams.

Spirit photography is a type of photography meant to capture images of ghosts and other spiritual entities. While currently employed in modern "ghost hunting," it has a strong history dating back to the late 19th century.

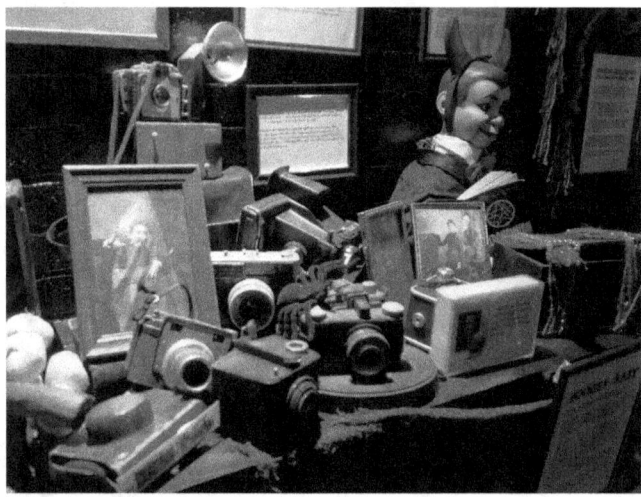

While many were hoaxes, some unexplained phenomenon in these photos have not been disproven.

One of the first voices in spirit photography was William H. Mumler in the 1860s. Mumler discovered the technique by accident, after he discovered a second person in a photograph he took of himself, which he found was actually a double exposure. Seeing there was a market for such images, Mumler started working as a medium, taking people's pictures and doctoring the negatives to add lost loved ones.

Mumler's fraud was discovered after he put identifiable living Boston residents in the photos as spirits.

While Mumler's photos were indeed fabrications, plenty of spirit photographs from this era have not been dismissed. In fact, the Crypt of Curiosities has been misfortunate enough to acquire two unique examples of the art form. On the next page are two brief descriptions.

Exhibit A (taken by A.E. Rupert) presents musician, Donald Lombardo, with a misty figure behind him. Lombardo believed this was the ghost of his late music teacher.

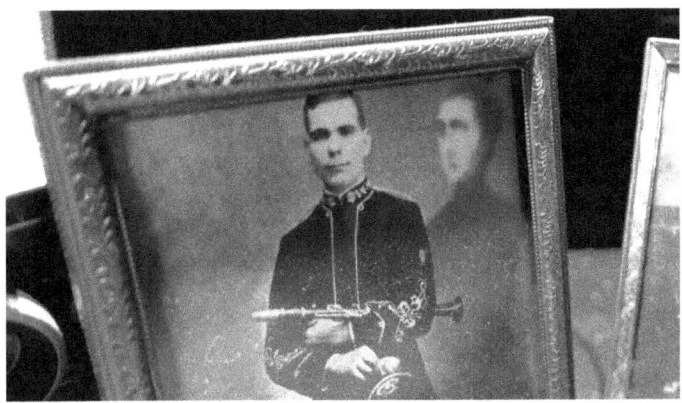

Exhibit B (taken by Oswald Coffax) shows young Miss Evelyn Bara, a wealthy New York socialite fascinated with the occult. Who's the mysterious specter lurking nearby? Historian believe it's Bara's Aunt Beatrice, who was killed in a terrible train collision years prior.

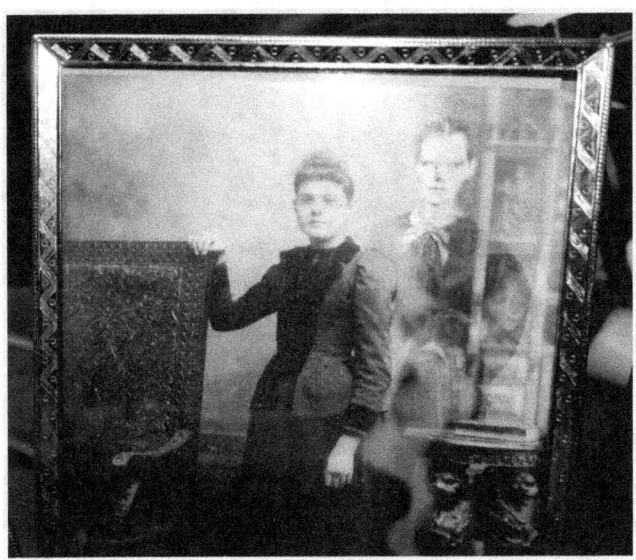

BOOGER BABY

The quaint town of Booger Hollow, Arkansas, isn't known for much except a two-story outhouse and this ghastly little infant.

The Booger Baby, as it came to be known, was discovered by hunter Rocky Dellman on a crisp autumn morning in late September of 1991. At first glance, Dellman perceived the poor child to be a large toad because of its green skin, but once he noticed its human anatomy, he immediately scooped it up and took it home to his wife Beth.

Rocky and Beth had been unable to conceive and saw this as a gift from the Lord above, but that original assessment couldn't be further from the truth.

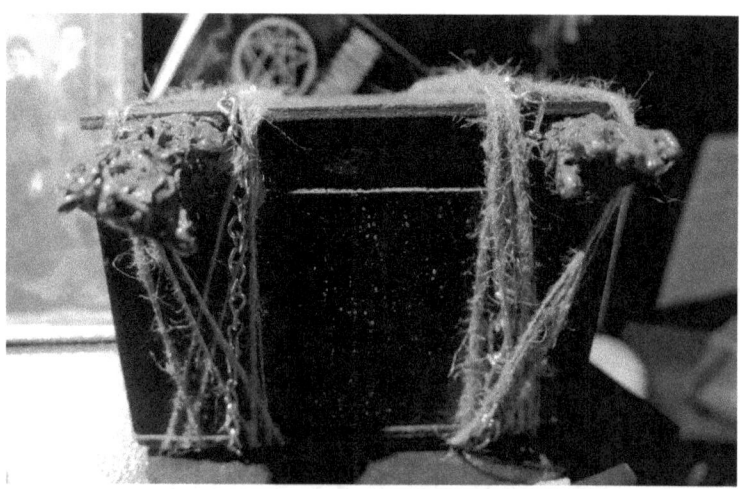

While nursing the child back to health, the foster parents sent for a doctor who gave them a shocking prognosis. The baby was no human at all. In fact, the doctor was not sure what it was...and neither were the Dellmans. The doctor pleaded with the Dellmans to give the creature to the local university for study, but they refused, citing that it would be immoral to do so. Instead, they kept him to raise as human, and that's when things became worse...

At first, it was just tiny bites on its foster parents' hands, but then the baby attacked and devoured their pet cat, Mr. Fluffy. The Dellmans had no other choice but to protect mankind from their adopted monster.

Rocky put the child in the box you see before you and chained it up. Not having the heart to murder the poor thing, he donated it to the Crypt of Curiosities shortly after the original incident.

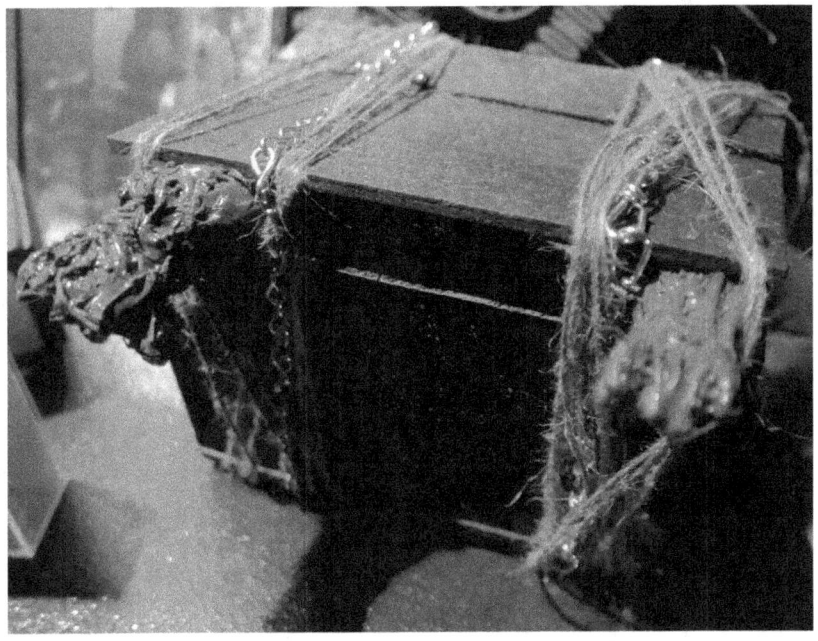

We kept him in storage until the Spring of 2017—hoping he would calm down a little.

VAMPIRE HUNTING KIT

Below is the personal vampire hunting kit of Dr. Luuk Meulenbelt, a quack physician who immigrated to the United States from Holland in the early 1920s.

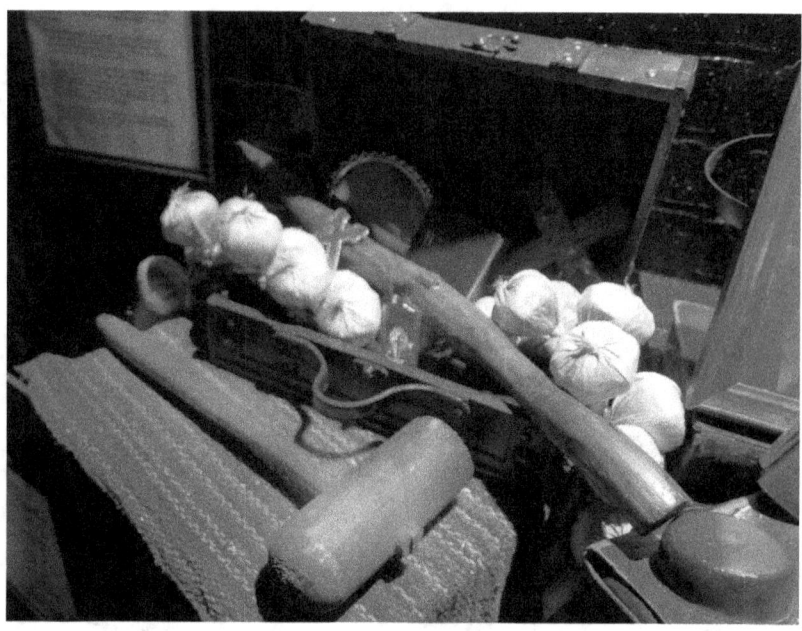

Meulenbelt was a firm believer in the undead and spoke proudly about the immense number of bloodsuckers he had exterminated in his homeland.

His American experience was less fruitful. Meulenbelt's only 'slaying' turned out to be a very much mortal young woman with a rare case of porphyria. The family was less than pleased with her obvious murder, and Meulenbelt was executed within a week of her death.

We acquired the sad doctor's partial vampire hunting kit in November 1989 from an auction. Some artifacts have been updated due to aging, including the garlic, as we do not wish to compromise the nasal integrity of the Crypt.

Here you'll see:

A **MIRROR** that the hunter held up to check for the lack of a reflection.

GARLIC that acted as a vampire repellant when the hunter wanted a little down time.

HOLY WATER that would make a vampire's skin boil at the smallest drop of this blessed liquid.

A **CRUCIFIX** that would force vampires to cower at its mere sight.

Once a vampire's identity was confirmed, driving a **STAKE** through its heart with the pounding of a **WOODEN MALLET** was the surefire way of taking it out.

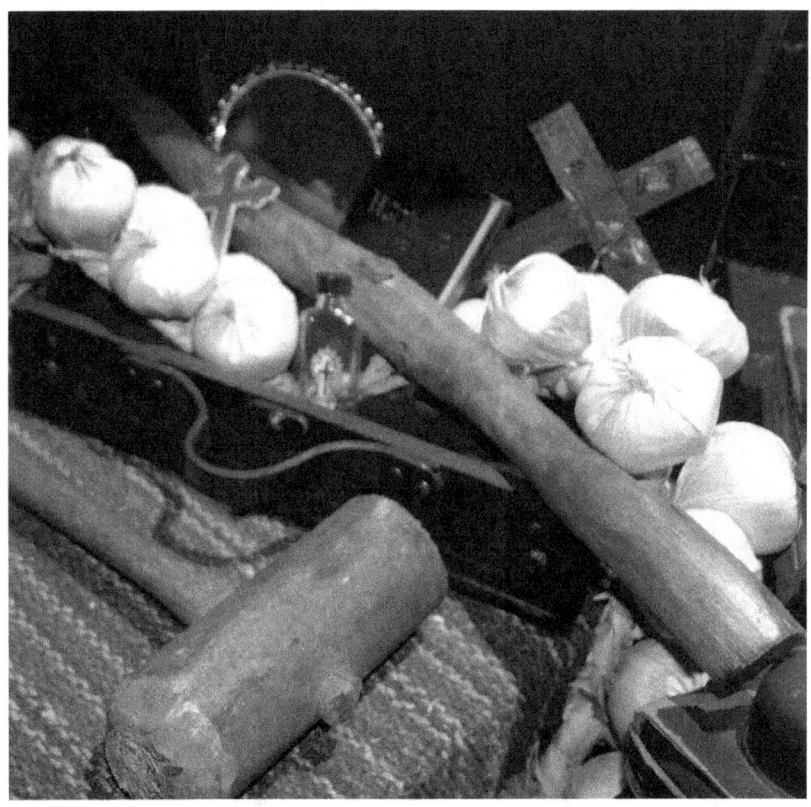

SCROLL OF ANUBUS

Some would call Professor Arthur Mulligan a crackpot for his wild theories on "resurrection ceremonies" and other peculiar rituals reportedly used to bring the dead back to life.

Mulligan was a professor at the now defunct Blessed Keeper Bible College in Tupelo, Mississippi. As the sole force behind the school's Archeology department, he held numerous lectures and seminars on his favorite subject —the re-animation of human tissue through the aid of religious ritual.

Before being fired from his position, Mulligan suggested that the return of Jesus Christ may have been made possible through the use of an ancient Egyptian document: the Scroll of Anubis.

The Scroll of Anubis was an almost mythical page of sorcery, frequently cited but never proven to actually exist.

The dean of Blessed Keeper Bible College was angered by Mulligan's blasphemous hypothesis and immediately demanded his resignation. Before Mulligan ended his tenure, he presented the dean with this rare artifact— supposedly the actual Scroll of Anubis.

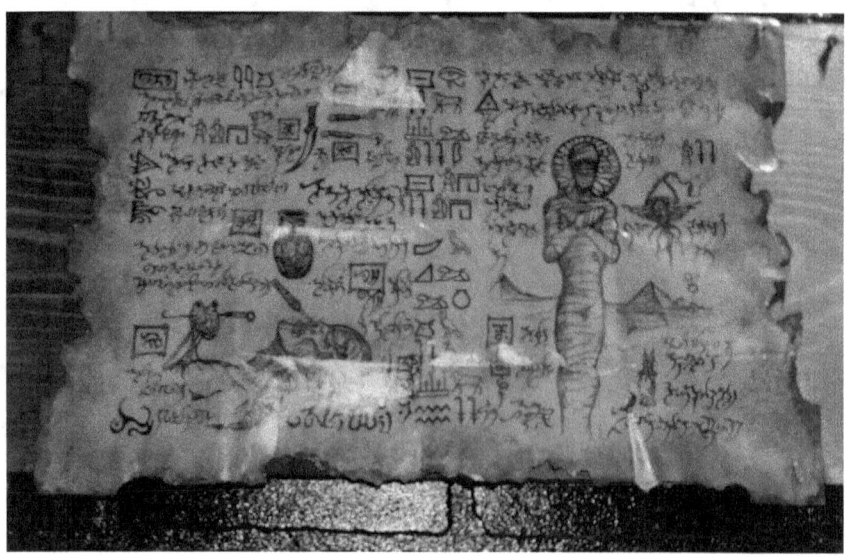

Furious, the dean spit on the weathered papyrus and slammed the door in Mulligan's face.

Two days later, the dean's office burned down. Fire fighters found the dean's corpse severely charred with signs that pieces of his brain had pulled out through his nose.

The only object in the fire that was left completely unharmed was the Scroll of Anubis.

The piece of papyrus remained in the possession of Tupelo fire fighter John Schroeder until his death in 1983, when his family donated his small library to a nearby thrift store.

The scroll itself was found stuffed in Schroeder's personal bible, right next to John 20:1.

Next to it was a newspaper article covering the fire and a few hand scribbled notes from Professor Mulligan.

When the book lot was purchased by Protean Books & Records owner Matt Beincewicz in 2015, he thought the scroll and its story would be an excellent addition to the Crypt.

GRIGORE
THE HIDEOUS BAT CHILD

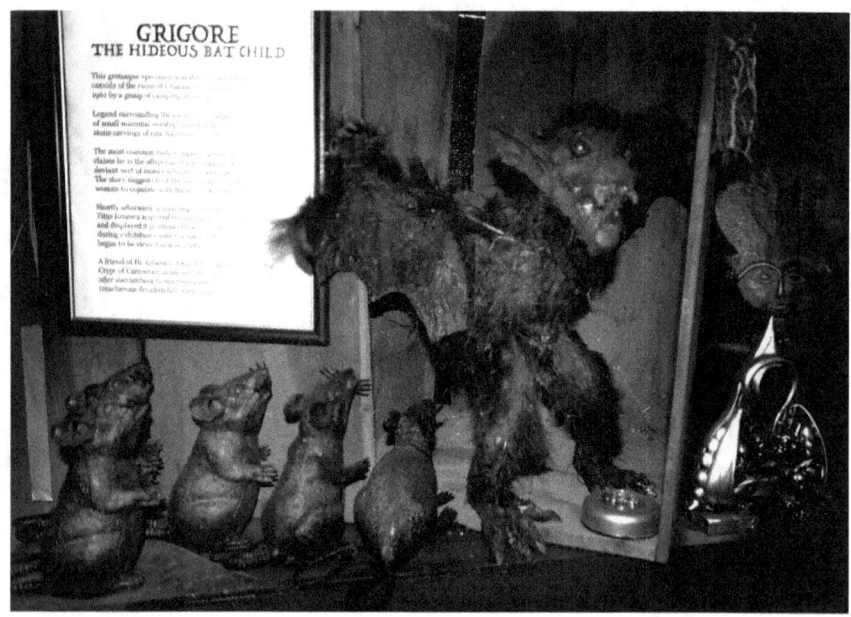

This grotesque specimen was discovered in the woods outside of the ruins of Chiajna Monastery in Bucharest in 1961 by a group of camping students.

Legend surrounding the monastery purports illegal sects of small mammal worship, proof of which was found in stone carvings of rats, hamsters, moles, and bats.

The most common rumor regarding Grigore the bat child claims he is the offspring of a teenage girl kidnapped by a deviant sect of monks who still worshipped at the ruins. The story suggests that the evil mystics forced the young woman to copulate with the spirit Rodescor, god of bats.

Shortly afterward, a traveling sideshow troupe leader, Titus Ionescu, acquired the corpse. Ionescu had it stuffed and displayed it prominently as part of his collection during exhibitions until the early 1980s, when such shows began to be viewed as distasteful.

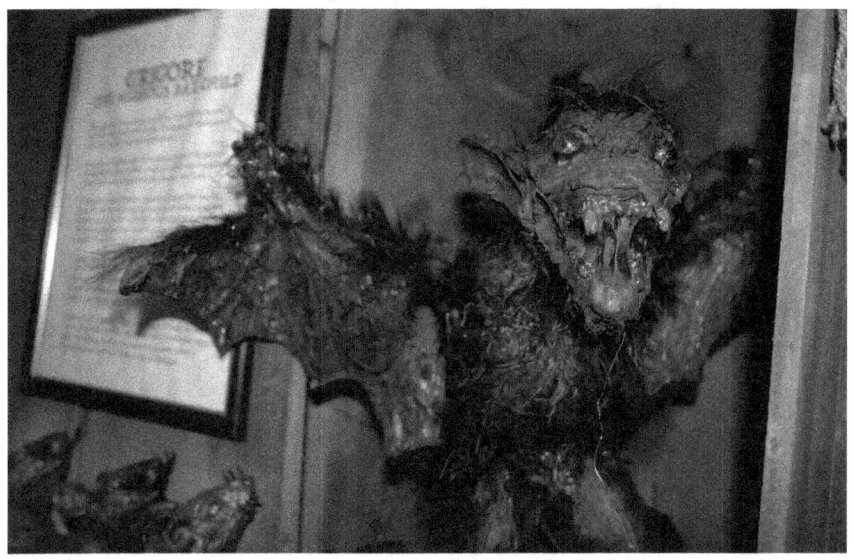

A friend of Dr. Gloom's, Titus left Grigore's body to the Crypt of Curiosities in his will. He died in November 1991 after succumbing to injuries caused by a particularly treacherous drunken fall down a spiral staircase.

STINGY JACK

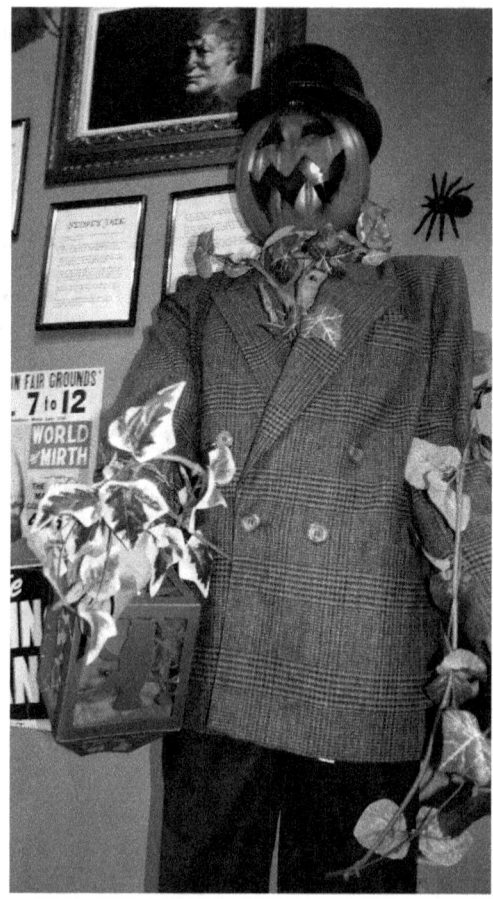

The story of the Jack O'Lantern goes back hundreds of years in Irish history.

Many of the stories, feature a miserable old drunk named Stingy Jack, who took pleasure in playing tricks on everyone: family, friends, and even the Devil himself.

One day, Jack tricked the Devil into climbing up a tree. Once the Devil was on a high branch, Stingy Jack swiftly placed crosses around the trunk of the tree.

Unable to touch a cross, the Devil was stuck. Stingy Jack made the Devil promise him not to take his soul when he died. Once the Devil promised not to take his soul, Stingy Jack removed the crosses, and the Devil climbed down.

Years later, when Jack died, he went to Heaven, where Saint Peter told Jack that he had lived a cruel, miserable life.

Stingy Jack was not allowed to enter Heaven, so he then went down to Hell. The Devil kept his promise and would not allow him to enter Hell.

He had nowhere to go but the dark Netherworld between Heaven and Hell. He asked the Devil how he could leave, as there was no light.

The Devil tossed him an ember from the flames of Hell to help Stingy Jack light his way. Jack had a turnip with him—it was one of his favorite foods, and he always carried one.

Jack hollowed out the turnip and placed the ember inside. From that day onward, Stingy Jack roamed the earth without a proper resting place, lighting his way with his "Jack O'Lantern."

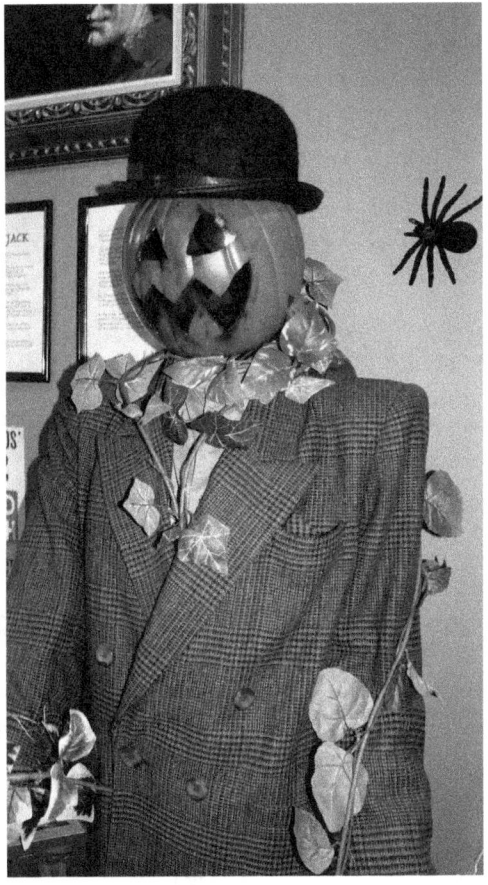

On All Hallow's Eve, the Irish hollowed out turnips, rutabagas, gourds, potatoes, and beets. They placed lights in them to ward off evil spirits.

In the 1800s, the first wave of Irish immigrants came to America. They quickly discovered that pumpkins were bigger and easier to carve, and so began the practice of using pumpkins for Jack O'Lanterns.

THE EYES OF A CLOWN

Be careful not to gaze too long at this eerie painting because the side effects can be deadly.

Since its creation in 1964 by artist Lloyd Shepard, dozens of observers have been driven to an early grave, and paranormal researchers have suggested it all comes back to this macabre piece of art.

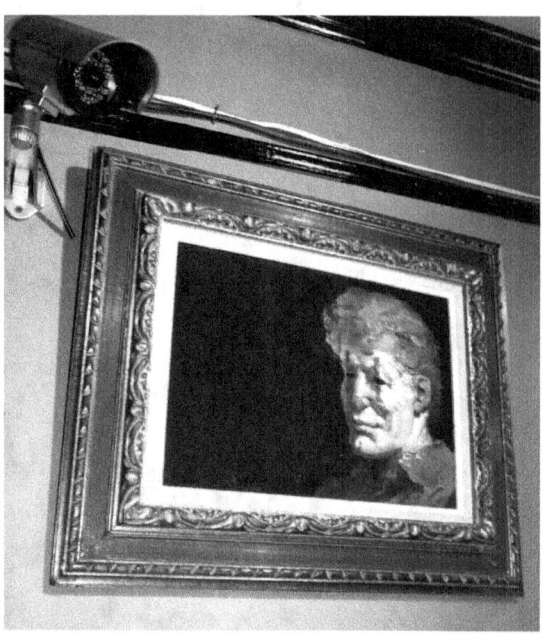

The painting, entitled *The Eyes of the Clown,* was the last piece that Shepard painted before his death.

Friends and family had voiced concern around Shepard's behavior during the last few months of his life. He had confessed to close associates that he had been haunted by visions of a "black-eyed jester." Shepard felt as if the grim harlequin was stalking him, but no one else witnessed what he had observed.

To get the morbid vision out of his head, Shepard set out to capture his tormentor on canvas. Shortly after the piece was finished, Shepard killed himself. His niece Claudia found his body in his studio. Both of his eyes had been stabbed with paint brushes.

Subsequent owners of the painting have made similar claims about the black-eyed clown following them after purchasing Shepard's masterpiece. Eight of the nine previous owners died shortly after acquiring the art. The ninth is currently a patient at Autumn Grove Mental Hospital.

FRISCO THE KILLER APE

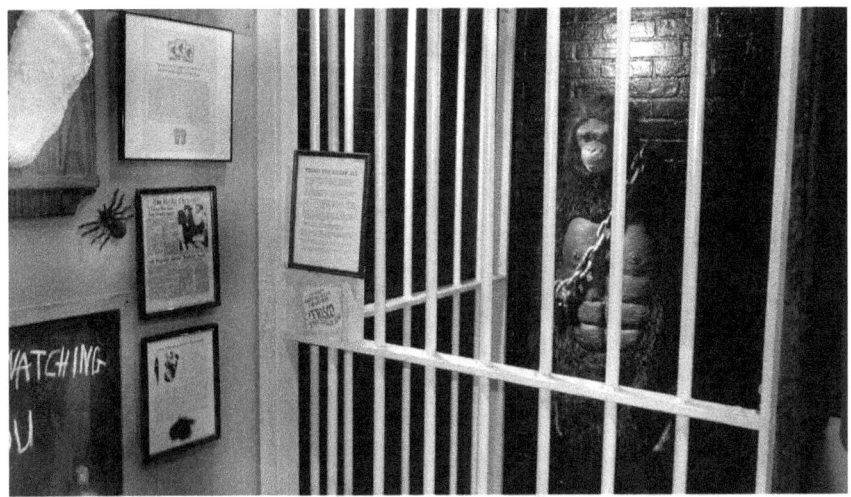

Our friend Frisco the ape met with an unfortunate end. He was slated to become the featured attraction at an amusement park that was the brain child of Orville Glut, a Baltimore carpet salesman.

Known as a cunning businessman, Mr. Glut decided to expand his small carpet business through a series of gimmicks. He wanted to fund an amusement park that would rival Coney Island.

He only needed a hook. Given the popularity of *King Kong*, it was clear that an ape would capture the imaginations of citizens young and old. Glut arranged to purchase a primate with hopes to present the animal in a grandiose gala event.

Glut had worked the sideshow circuit when he was younger and knew how to create buzz while also impressing the deep pockets of Baltimore's social elite. He arranged a huge black tie event and even had a tailor create a suit for Frisco.

Tragedy struck when some of the attendees drank a bit too much of the free-flowing champagne and started to taunt Frisco.

Scared, alone, and confused, Frisco snapped and escaped his binding. Glut was one of those attacked; he died at the hands of his own money-making scheme.

The Frisco seen here is a recreation. The real Frisco was detained shortly after the massacre and sold to a zoo in St. Louis.

When visiting the Crypt, we encourage visitors to step inside the prison cell and take pictures… but please, do not taunt him.

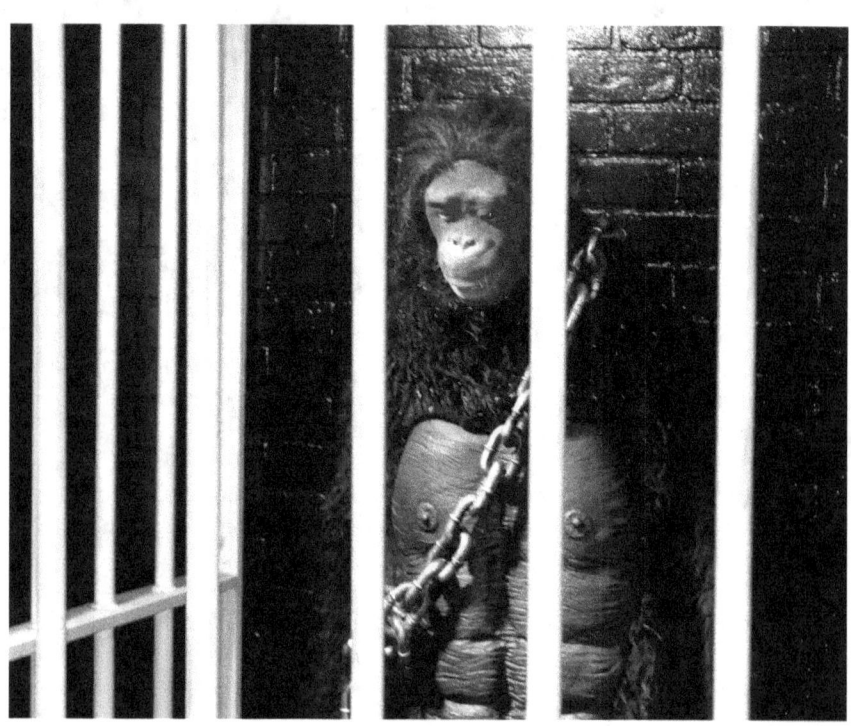

SLATE WRITING

Slate writing is a means of spirit communication that started during the heyday of Spiritualism and continued into the middle 20th century.

It involves alleged psychic ability allowing a person to produce written words without consciously writing. The words are claimed to arise from a subconscious, spiritual, or supernatural source.

In spiritualism, spirits are claimed to take control of the hand of a medium to write messages, letters, and even entire books.

This particular slate was donated to the museum by Ms. Judith Windell. It belonged to her late grandfather, Professor Everett Clayton Gauntheim. A man of significant note in the Spiritualist movement, Gauntheim conducted many channeling sessions during his tenure in the Psychology department of Adamson University.

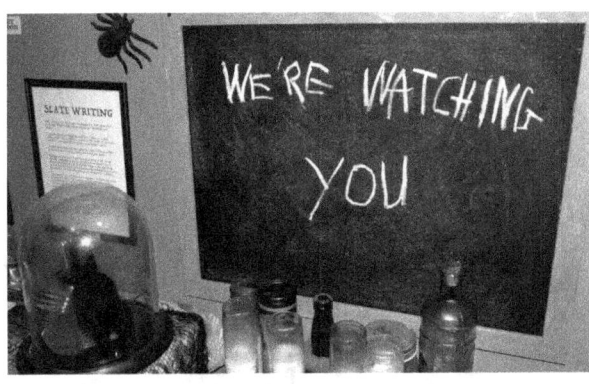

Most notably, one of Gauntheim's colleagues— a gentleman who'd committed suicide — used the slate to send messages from beyond the grave.

Early transmissions lead police to the discovery of his body and allowed his family to communicate with the deceased to coordinate funeral arrangements.

To this day, strange messages will often show up on the very slate.

Most are cheerful greetings from joyful spirits on the other side, but every once in a while, something sinister has shown up.

Tread lightly, dear friends. Some of the dead resent the mere breath of the living.

'SʔUATCH NESS
MONSTER

It may not look like it, but this is supposedly the offspring of interspecies fornication between the Loch Ness Monster and Bigfoot herself.

This little runt was apparently saved from a litter of similar creatures on the muddy banks of Loch Ness on a foggy morning in March 1981. The gentlemen who found them—a surly champ by the name of Jack Campbell —was a well-known pool shark whose penchant for alcohol often lead him to harass the general populace residing near the lake.

Campbell infamously bragged that he made the discovery while he was "three sheets to the wind." Upon scooping up this furry little critter, he heard the throaty shrieks of its mother from the nearby brush.

Campbell held on tight to the delicate baby creature as he ran for his life, but his grip was too tight. In fact, he inadvertently strangled the little beast and by the time he returned to the scene, all he found was the enormous foot prints of the lady Sasquatch.

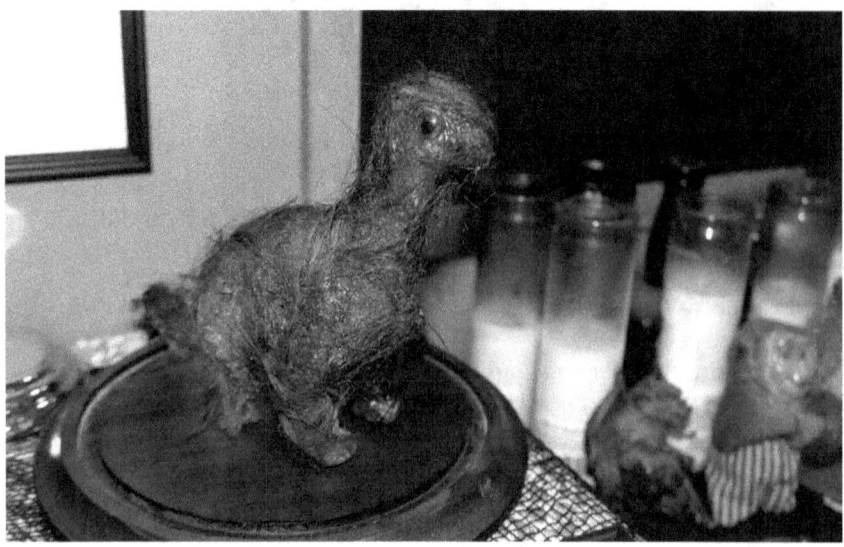

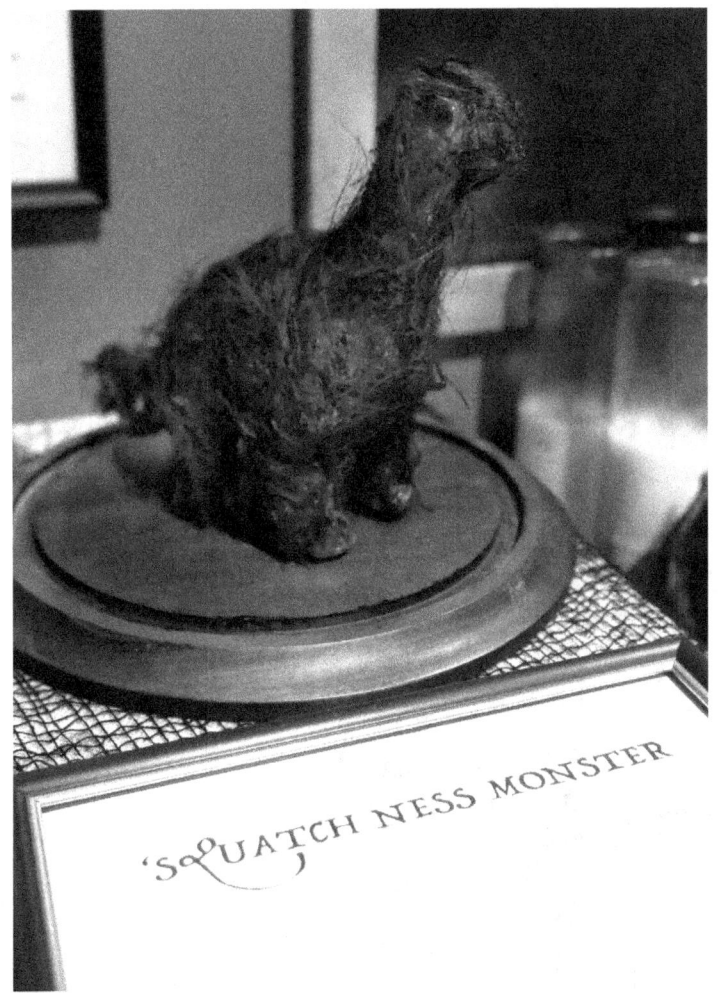

'SQUATCH NESS MONSTER

Hoping to profit from the whole fiasco, Campbell had the baby stuffed and planned to sell it to a local dime museum, but his sneaky reputation destroyed those prospects for Campbell.

Believing the piece to be a "gaff," every sale fell through and Jack Campbell was forced to keep the kooky critter in his personal possession until 2016, when a representative from the Crypt purchased it from Campbell's estate after he died from liver failure in December 2015.

Editors' Note: There have been no reported sightings of Bigfoot near Loch Ness outside of Mr. Campbell's claims.

THE PENNY MAN

Throughout history, coins have been placed on the eyes of the deceased during funeral services.

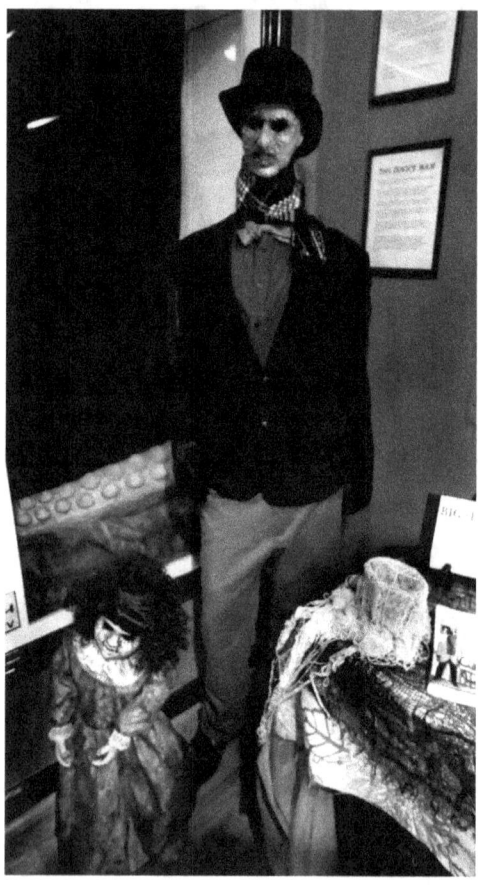

Some say it's a simple trick used to keep eyelids from popping open during the funeral, but others profess that the copper pennies are used as viaticum: provisions for the journey.

This strange "funeral toll" is part of a mythology that advises a fare must be paid so that a soul may pass on to the afterlife.

Legend has it that those on the pilgrimage to the other side will meet a guardian with burnt holes for eyes and hands as cold and clammy as those of a corpse.

It's been said that the well-dressed gentlemen will greet a you wearing a grim expression but will break into a sardonic smile at the tinkling knell of coins. This entity is known as the Penny Man.

Folklore suggests the Penny Man can guarantee safe travel into the afterlife, shepherding the departed through the murkiness of the river Styx. He is unconcerned with what befalls the passenger upon arrival at the land of the dead; he has his payment and eagerly awaits his next customer.

THIRD NIPPLE OF ELVIS PRESLEY

Here at the Crypt, we were all shook up when we came across this most unusual piece.

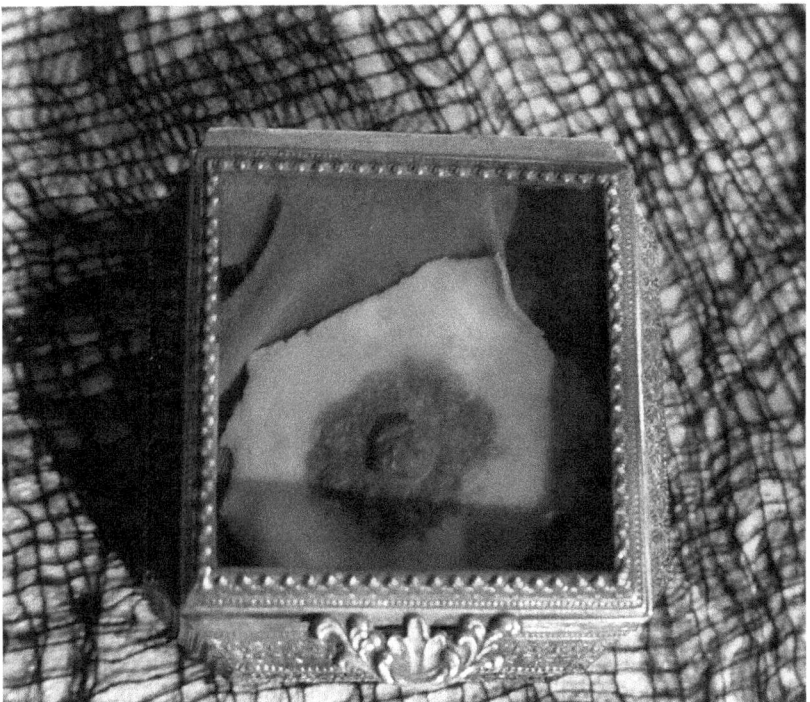

It is a well-guarded fact that the notorious "King of Rock-n-Roll" Elvis Presley had three nipples prior to his enlistment in the U.S. army. Moments before the iconic snapshot of his physical exam was taken, military doctors severed young Elvis's third teat in the hopes that the tabloid press would not torment the poor musician for his minor medical affliction.

Suspicious minds may be curious how this nipple came into our possession.

Well, here's the truth:

A young nurse couldn't help falling in love with the King's cut-off bosom and kept it in her personal possession for nearly four decades before it came to our attention.

Sure, it was a little odd, but don't be cruel. The woman loved Elvis's music, and his nipple proved a truly unique reminder of her chance meeting with the celebrity.

Upon the nurse's death, a family member (who wishes to remain anonymous) sold us the nipple for a modest sum.

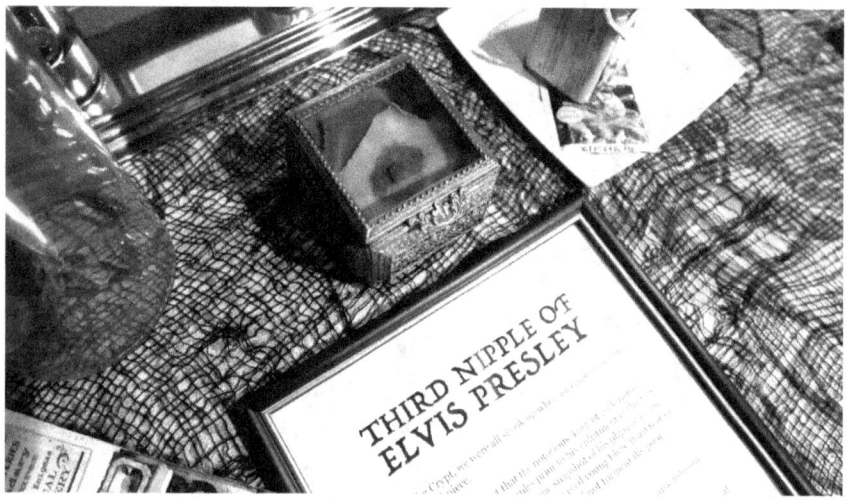

Elvis may have "left the building," but his third nipple remains with us.

PENANGGALAN

Found in Southeast Asia, the Penanggalan is a ravenous creature, understood to be a transformed female midwife who broke a pact with the Devil. As punishment, she is forced to feed on the blood of newborn babies.

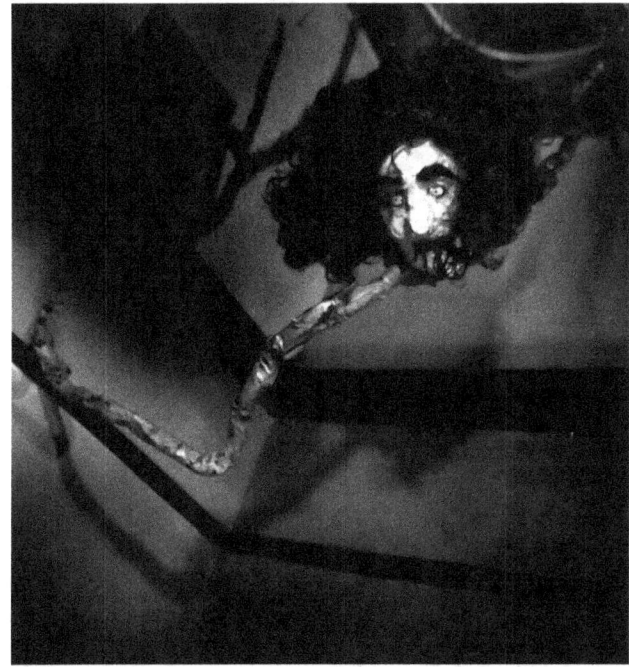

Not your traditional vampire, the head of the Penanggalan detaches and flies through the night sky, dangling its wet entrails behind it as it seeks out an unwitting victim. The unfortunate souls upon whom the demon feeds suffer from wasting diseases and open sores that almost always prove fatal.

The head displayed here at the Crypt of Curiosities was modeled on an actual severed head belonging to a midwife from Malaysia named Rubini.

Her attempts to drink from a girl in town were thwarted by the thorny vines surrounding the girl's dwelling. The lungs and intestines hanging from Rubini's gaping neck caught in the trap and held her captive until morning, when she was discovered dead by the girl's father.

Her death came as a result of her being unable to reattach to her body by sunrise.

Y'KNOW WHAT THEY SAY ABOUT BIG FEET...

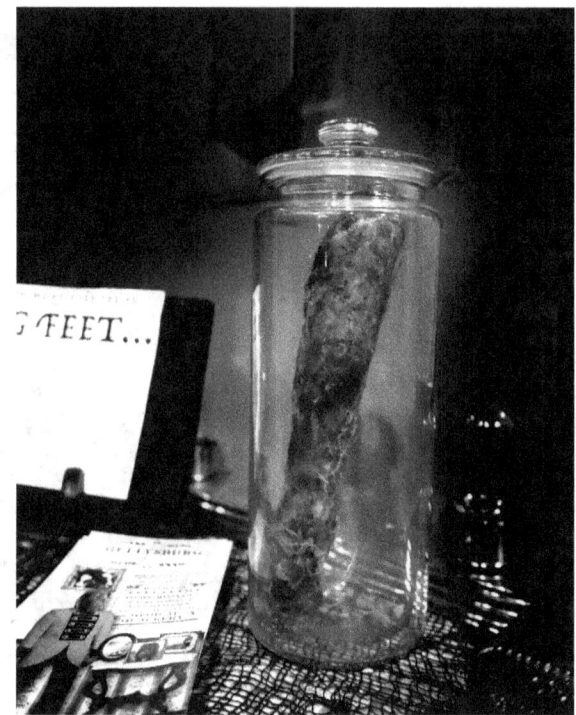

This peculiar appendage was unearthed near Bluff Creek, California, not far from the location where the infamous Patterson-Gimlin Bigfoot footage was filmed.

Originally, novice hiker Ronald J. Holmes believed it to be some sort of primitive tool or fossilized wood, but he wasn't sure, so he took the strange object to his local university.

After much scrutiny, biology professor L.D. Silver came to believe it was a member of the Sasquatch family—a phallus, actually, from some sort of hairy, bipedal humanoid. Professor Silver kept the item for many years until he retired in 2007. That's when the item inched its way to the Crypt.

SEVERED TENTACLE OF TINTAMARRE

The French island of Tintamarre currently has no human inhabitants, but from 1946 to 1950 it was used as a base for the airline Compagnie Aerienne Antillaise.

Prior to their departure from business on the island, the airline's management had noticed a rash of deadly natural disasters on the southern end of the island. There was massive flooding, trees were uprooted, and small animals were found strangled and suffocated.

Retired sailor Jacques Fournier was the last resident of the island. Fournier claims to have drunkenly battled in 1953 an enormous octopus he described as "terrifiante" and unusually "degoutant."

With the aid of a broken wine bottle, Fournier severed a single tentacle from the vile sea creature and dragged it home to his hut. His hope was that the putrid trophy could be used as evidence of his near fatal encounter.

Weeks later when he returned to mainland France, no researcher could place the biological make-up of the beast. Proud and satisfied with its rarity, Fournier had it stuffed and mounted on his wall.

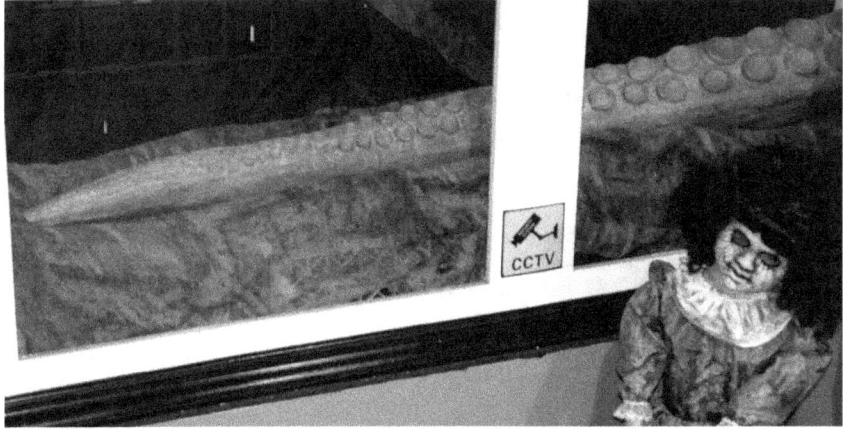

Upon Fournier's death, the tentacle was donated to the Crypt by his boyfriend in June of 1962.

THE MONKEY'S PAW

Perhaps you've heard of W.W. Jacobs's terrifying short story first published in 1902, but what if you knew the supernatural power of a severed monkey's paw was real?

Since the mid-18th century, seekers of the unusual have shared disturbing first-hand accounts of men and women who have tempted fate through dangerous wishes made on paws just like this one.

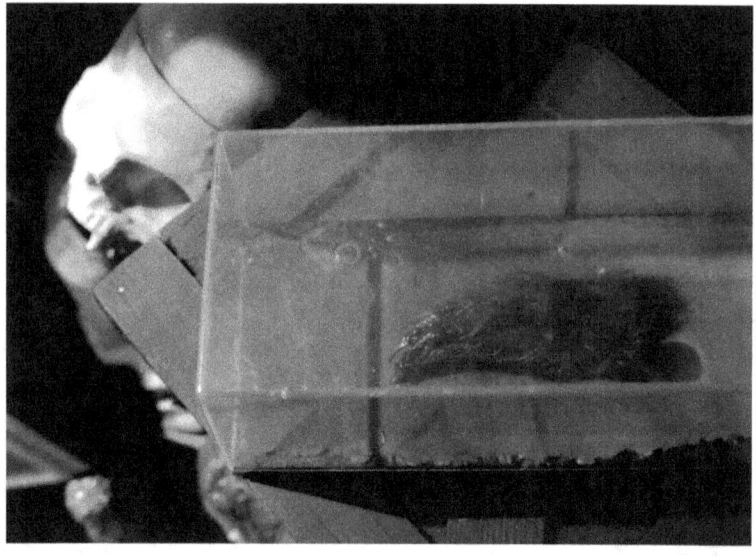

This meager furry hand is one of those evil tools that leads to worry and ruin. Every encounter brings terrifying unintended consequences to fools who do not know its mystical powers.

Each owner of the monkey's paw is entitled to three wishes, but these requests never come easily. Instead, each ask turns out horribly different than expected and often leads to misfortune or even death.

We ask each visitor to respect *our wishes* and do not touch or ask the monkey's paw for anything at all.

AVENGING GHOST CRAB

(Callinectes Vindicates - Translation: Beautiful Deadly Swimmer)

From Locust Point to Essex and all along the Delmarva coastline, the decades-old legend of the Ghost Crab has struck fear in the hearts of many a horny teenager.

Young lovers from Ocean City to Fells Point report waking up with mysterious hickeys and no memory of the cause. Citing their high blood alcohol level, many believed it was from a drunken tryst that they couldn't recall, but local marine biologists believe the bites are that of a decapod crustacean.

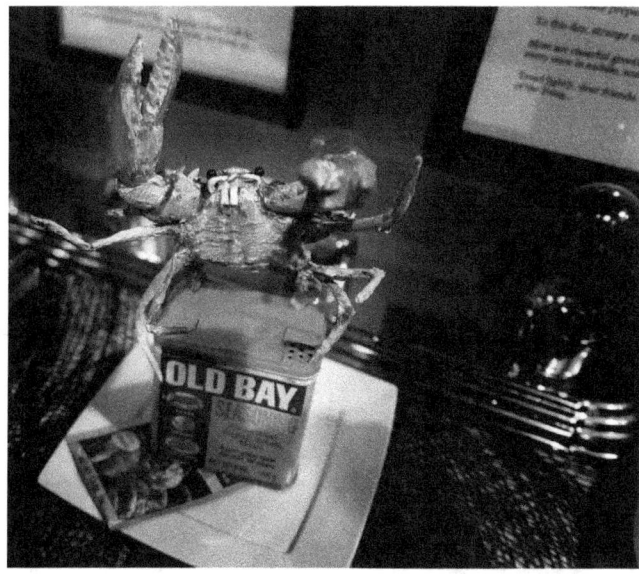

Why does this phantom sea creature stop at mere bites?

Baltimore folklore suggests that the Ghost Crab is repelled by alcohol and can feast no further on a human who has indulged in liquor.

Rumors suggest that the seasoning Old Bay, on the other hand, makes the Crab more fierce and powerful.

Beware, dear friends! The Avenging Ghost Crab is out of the bushel and he wants food… So drink up!

POPALON

Ever see a lonely single shoe on the side of the highway?

Originating in Belfast, the story of the Popalon spread throughout Europe over centuries. Small in stature, but big in brains, the Popalons were mischievous creatures who stole from hard-working humans. It was said that they lived in holes off the sides of roads, waiting for carriages to stop for rest or lose cargo as they passed by.

While their motivations were unknown, it seemed that their preferred loot was items of clothing. The mythos evolved evolved to include the hearing of song and dance from the creatures after a "good haul." While this legend cannot be verified, the only definite pattern of behavior is a preference for the stealing of footwear over any other garment.

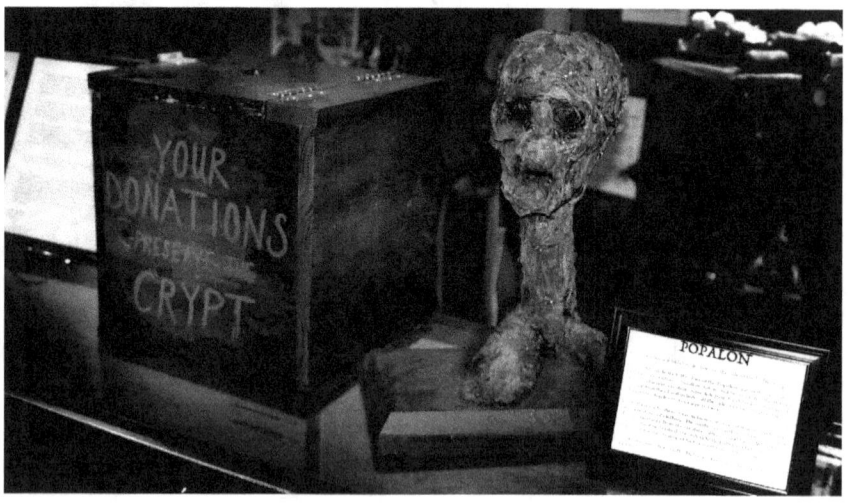

So, why the "one shoe" on the highway? Popalons, you see, have two <u>left</u> feet.

GALLERY

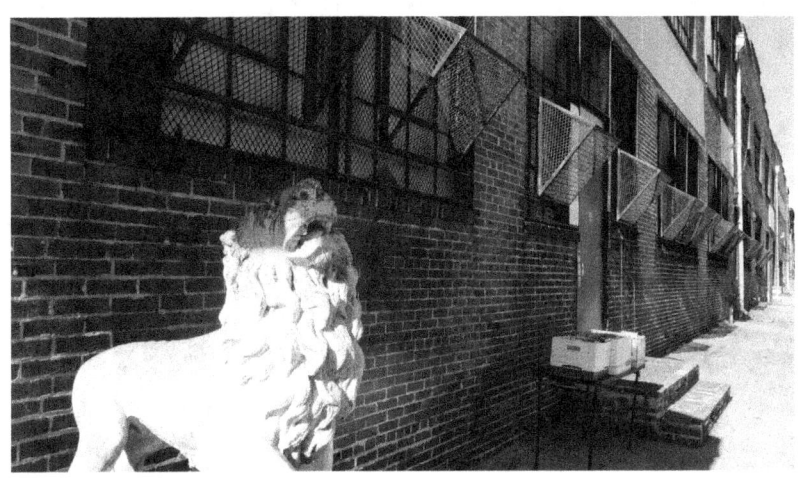

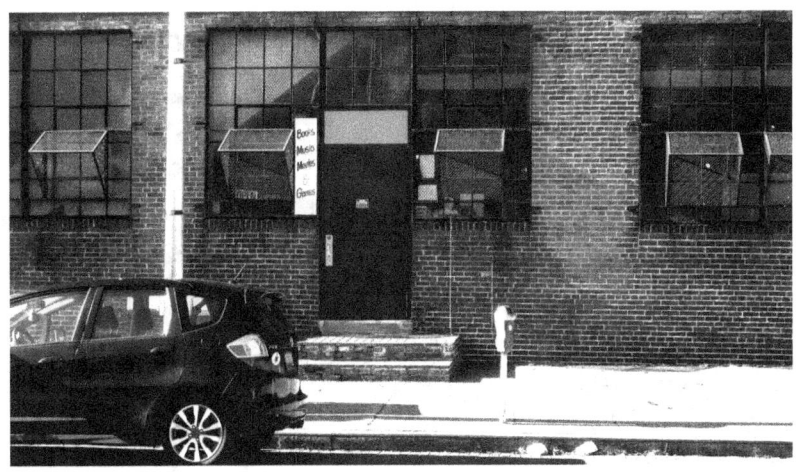

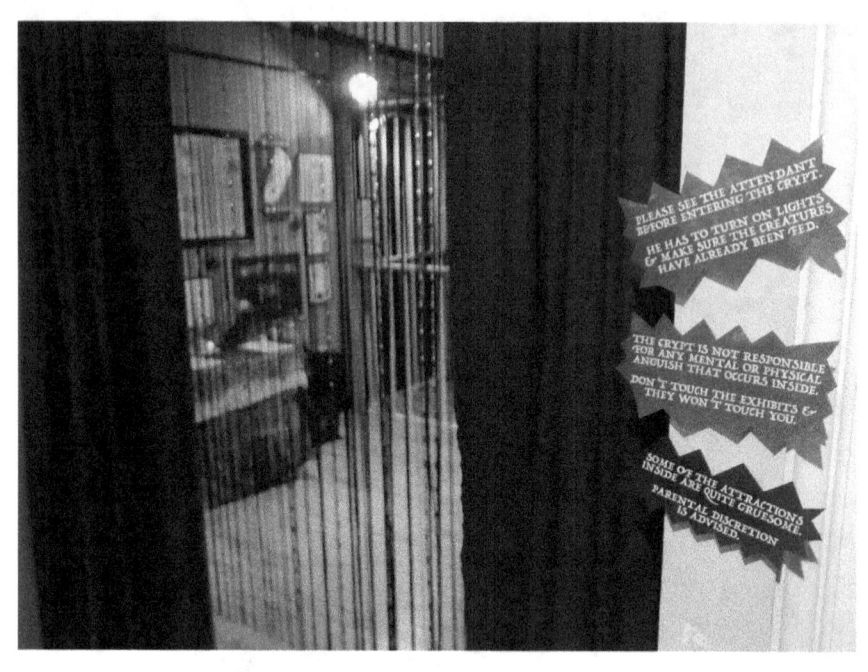

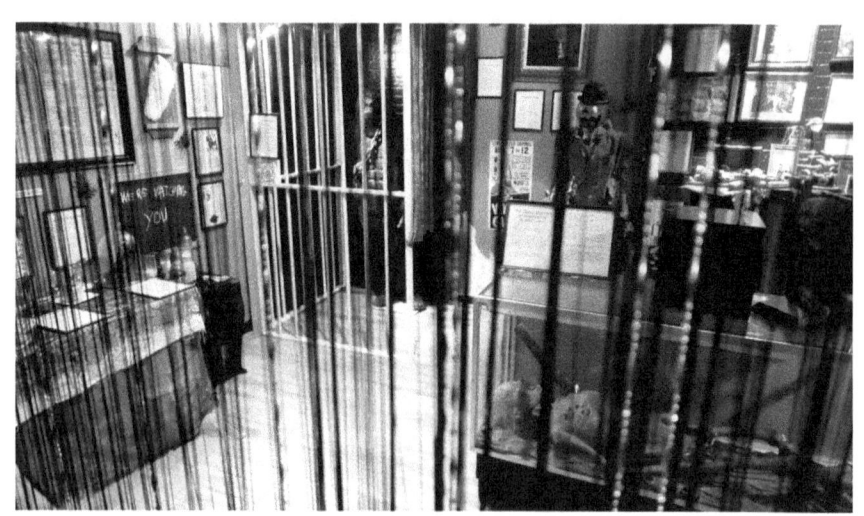

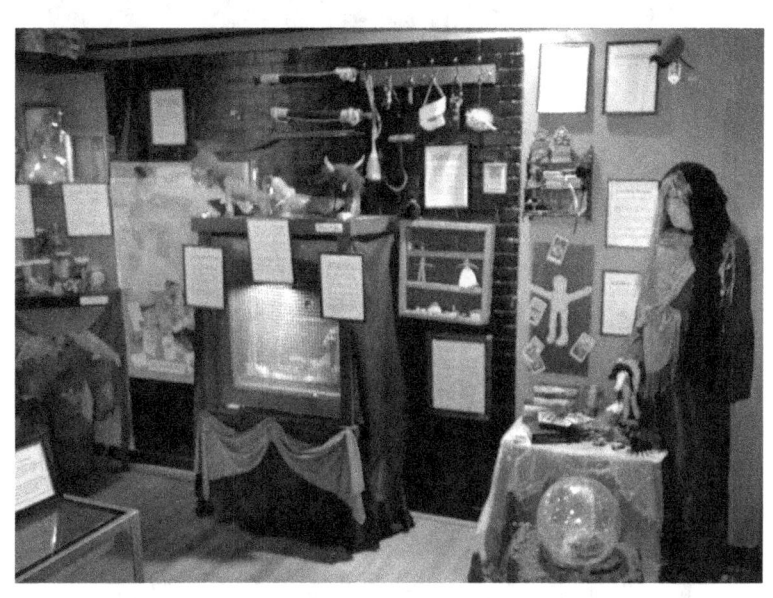

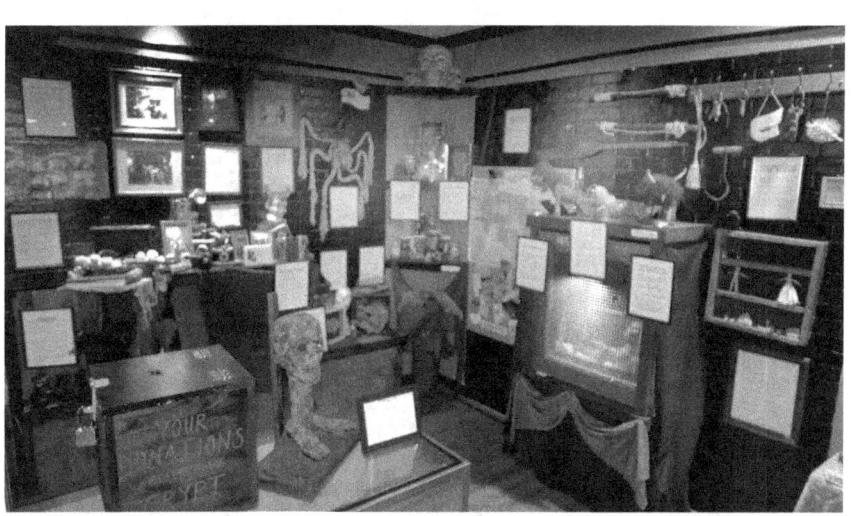

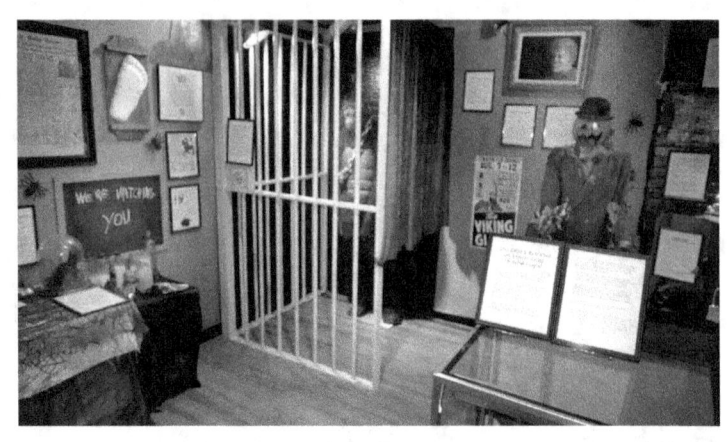

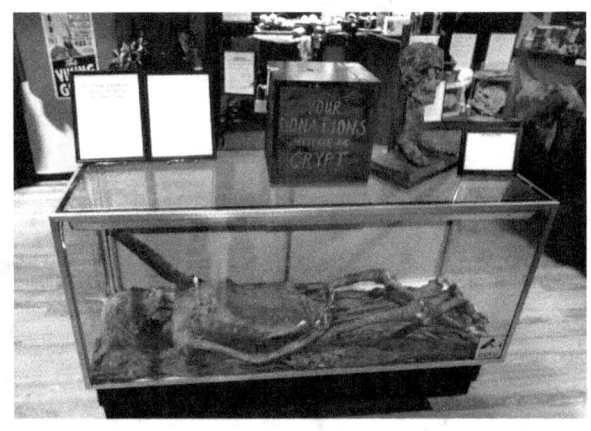

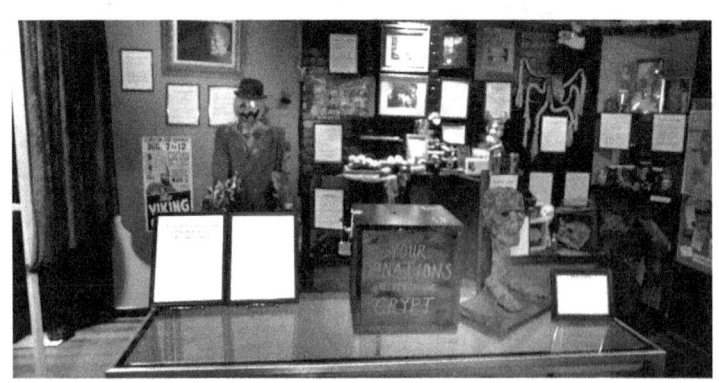

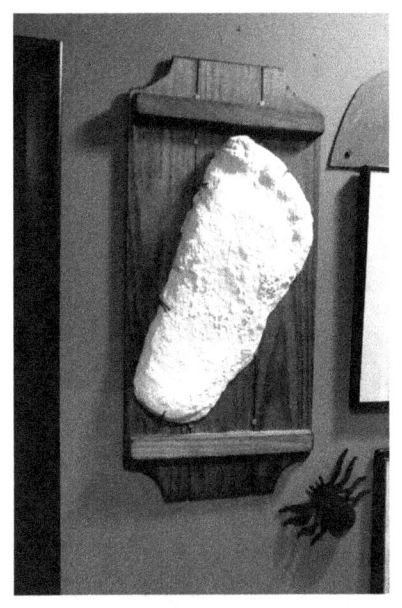
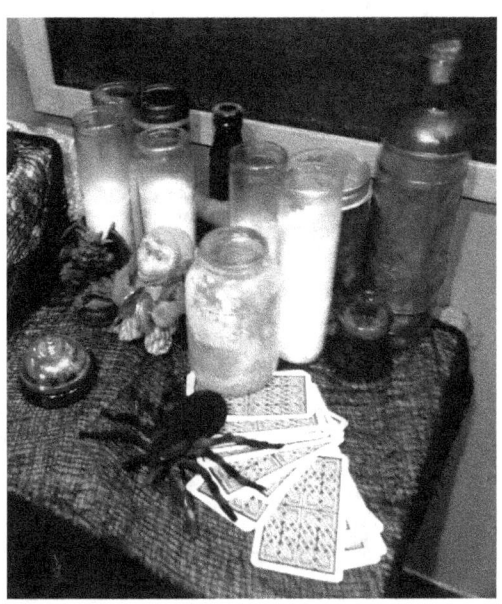

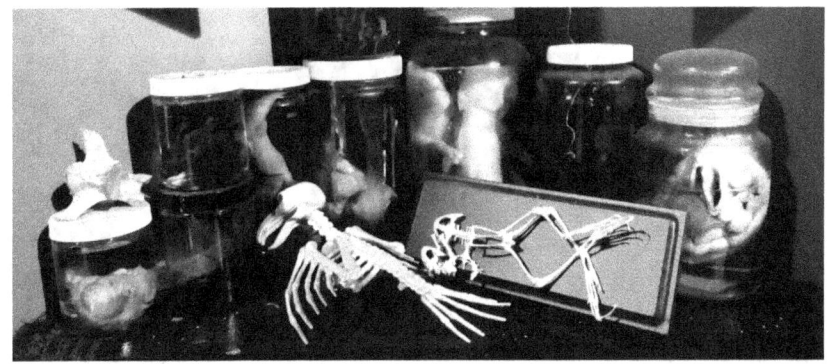

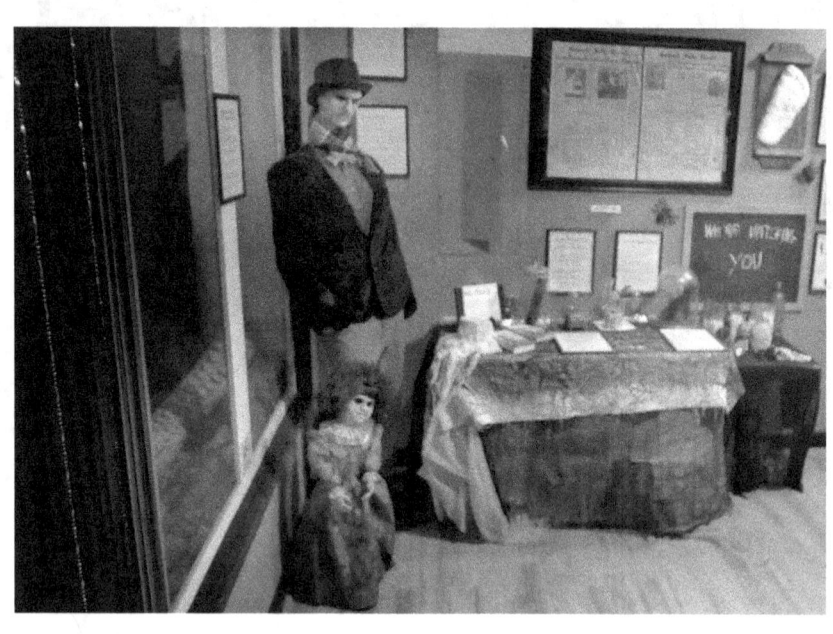

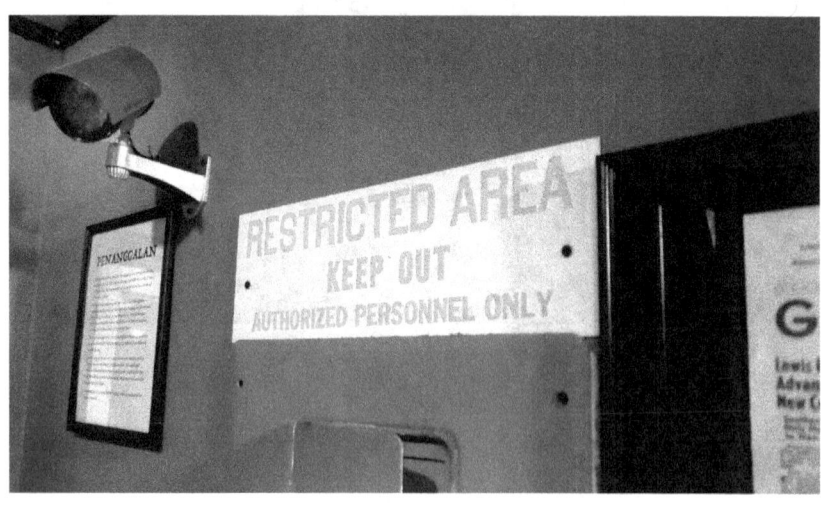

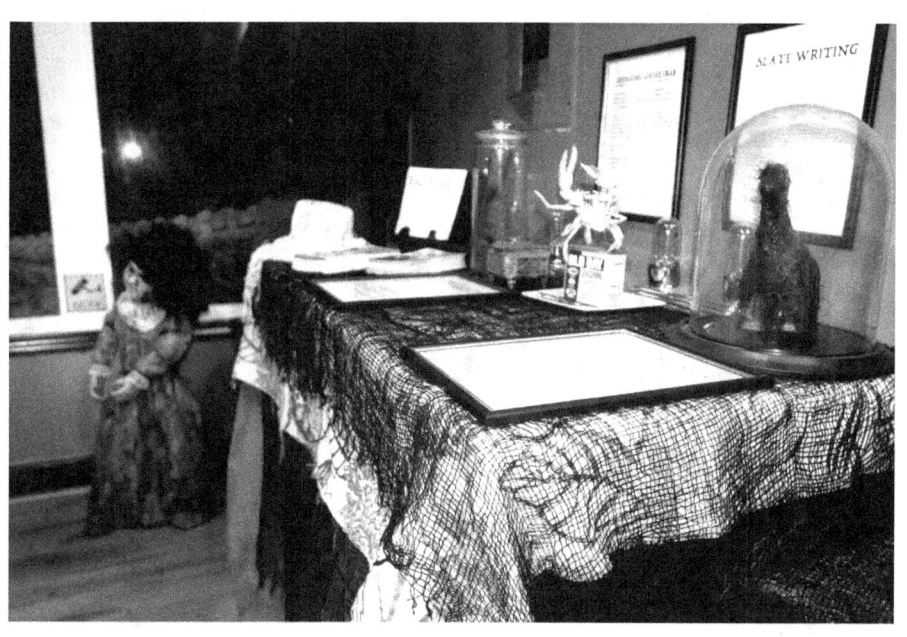

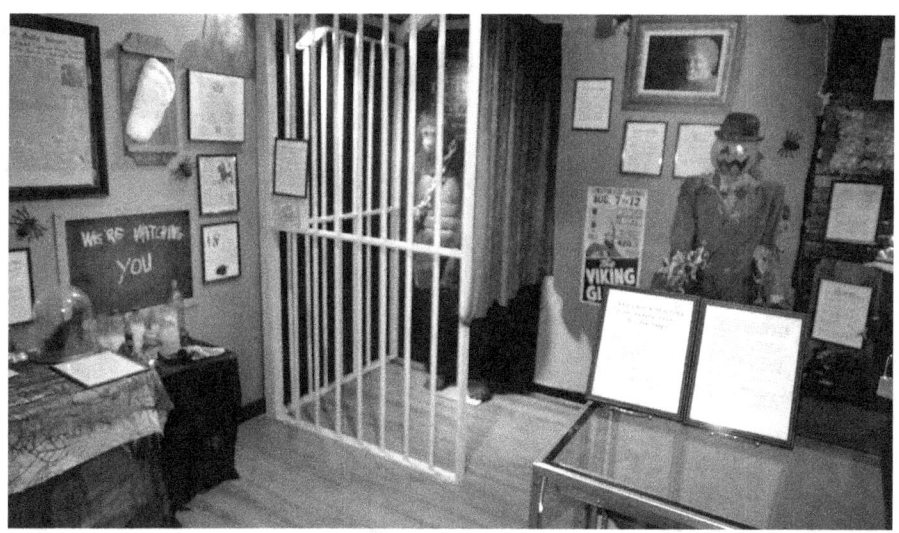

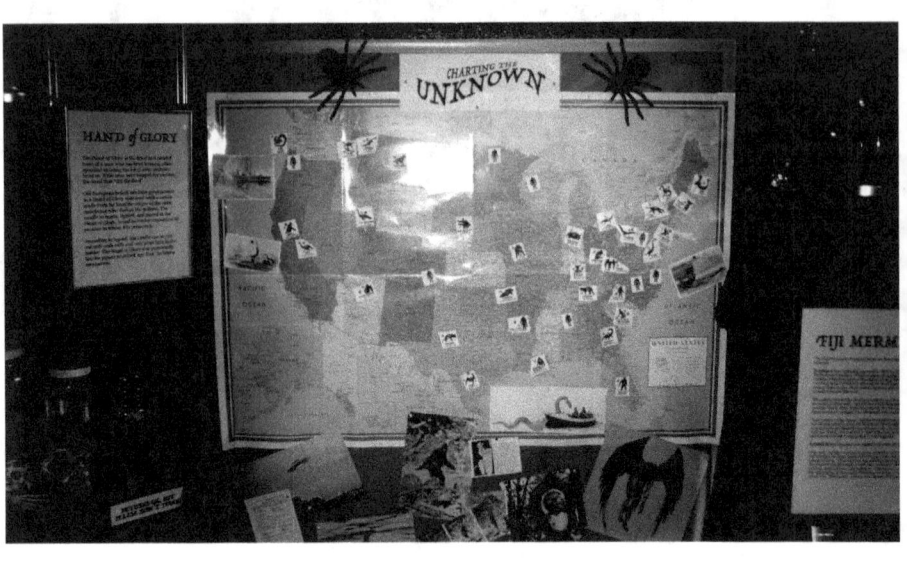

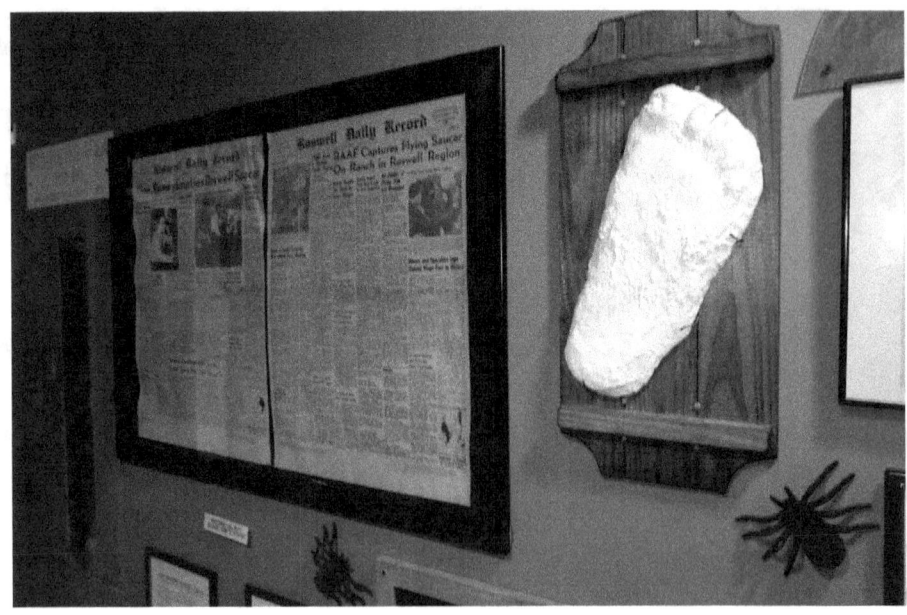

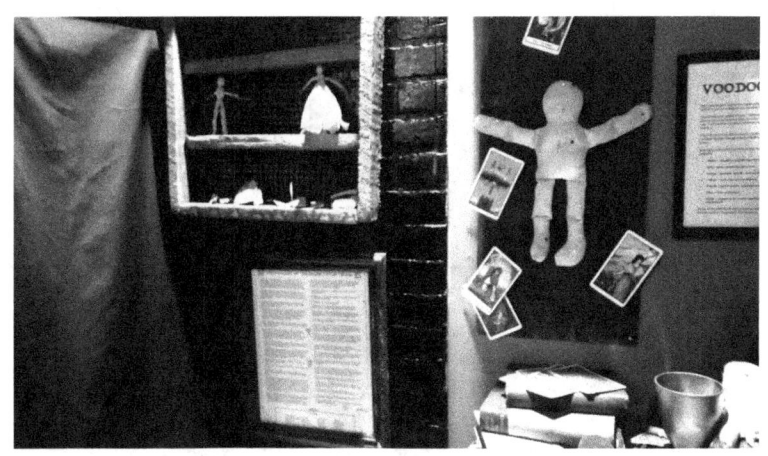

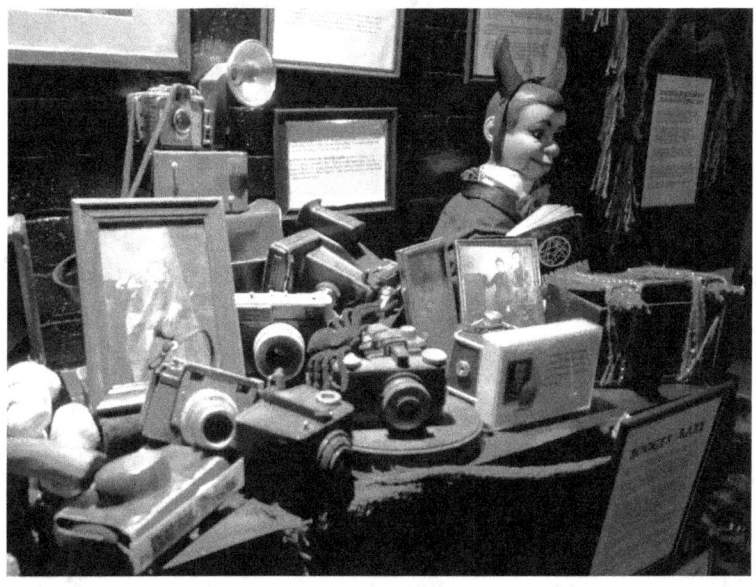

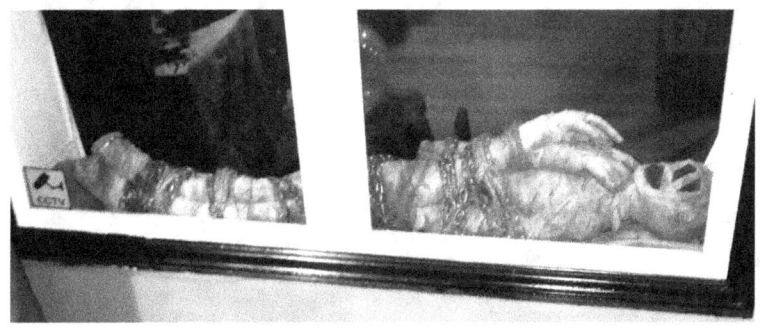

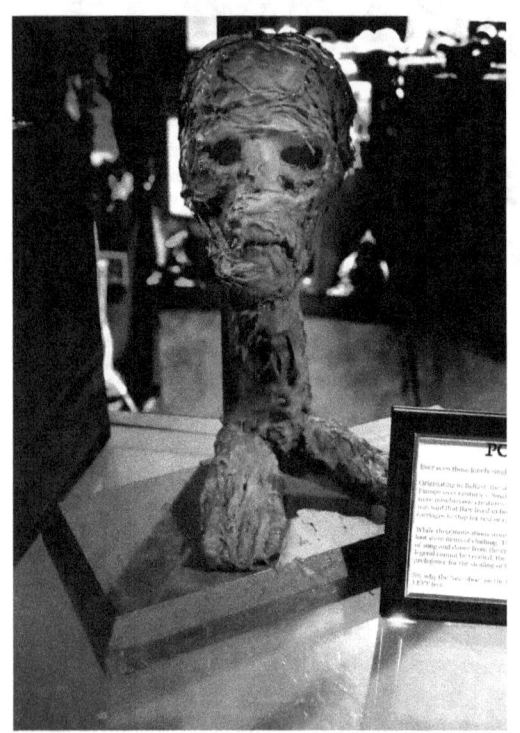

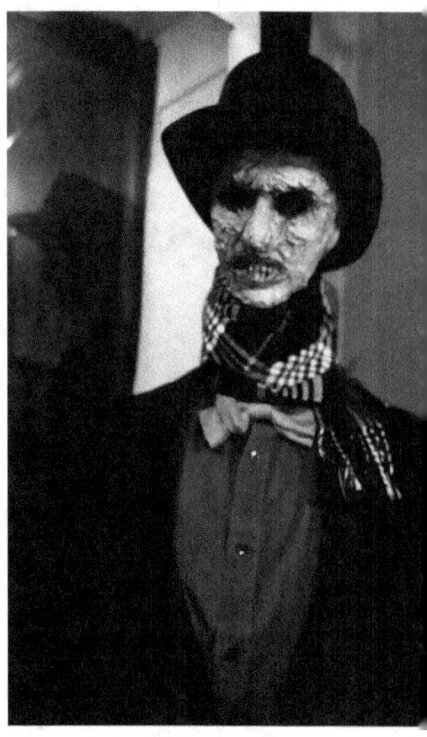

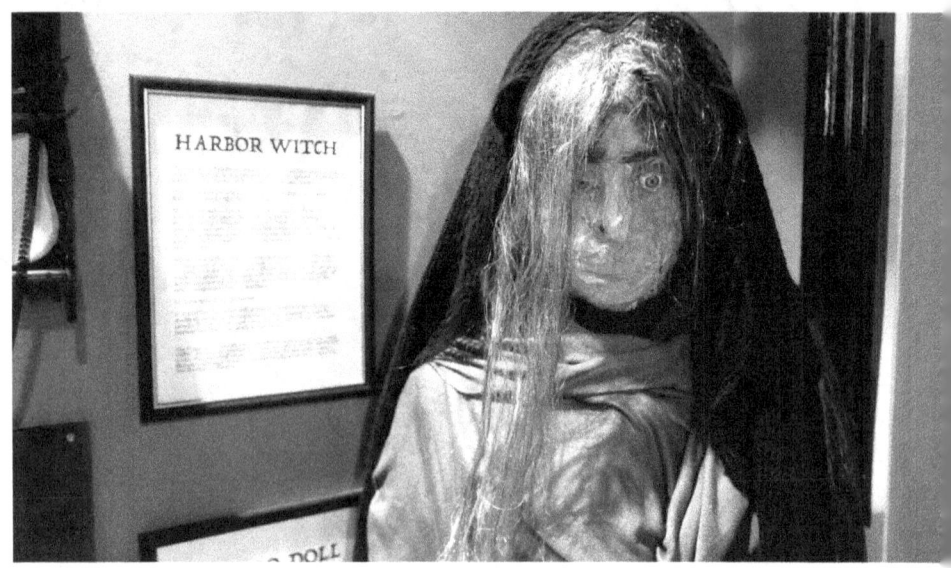

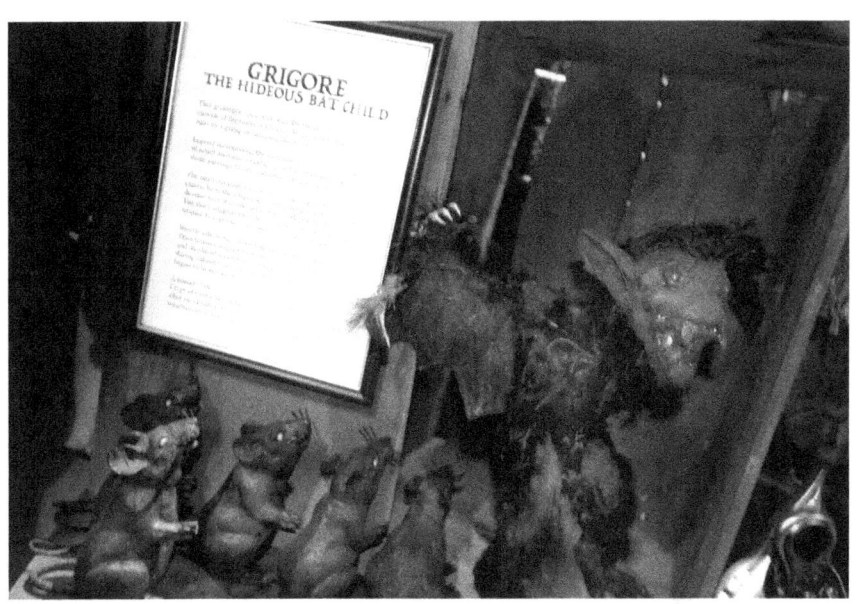

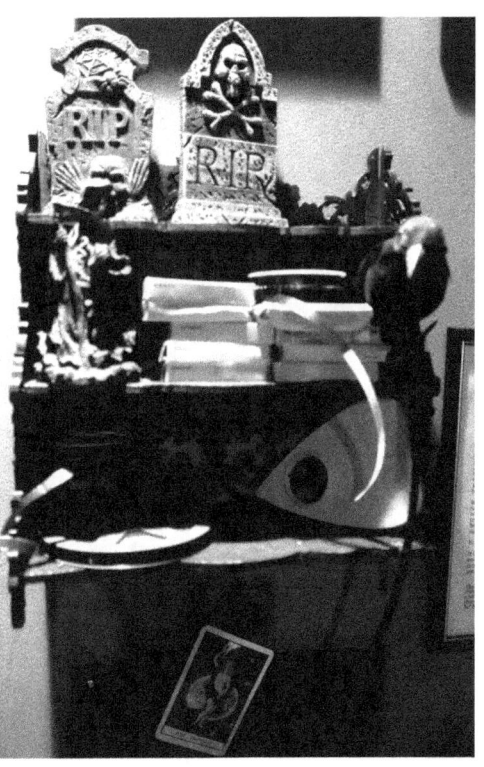

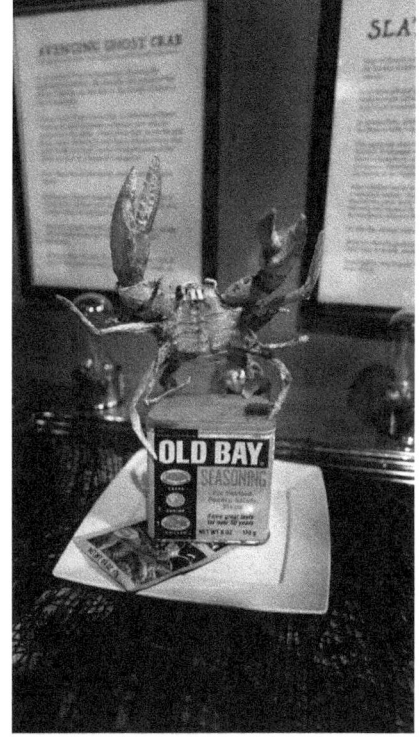

www.ingramcontent.com/pod-product-compliance
Lightning Source LLC
Chambersburg PA
CBHW051331220526
45468CB00004B/1596